Mystics

THE BEAUTY OF PRAYER

columba press

23 Merrion Square North, Dublin 2
www. columba.ie

First published in 2016 by FitzBeck Publishing

Original Title: *An Inner Music, Living a Life in God*

This edition, published in 2018 by Columba Press

Cover design by Alba Esteban | Columba Press

Book design by Alba Esteban & Maria Soto | Columba Press

Photography: Courtesy of St Mary of the Angels, Wellington
– the church where Craig Larkin was ordained 1 July, 1967.
Caryll Houselander photograph, University of Notre Dame Archives

ISBN 978-1-78218-327-3

Printed by L&C Poland

THE BEAUTY OF PRAYER

CRAIG LARKIN SM

COLUMBA PRESS

CONTENTS

FOREWORD

To have written a book is not a small thing – and Craig Larkin has authored several books. But to have distilled so much of his accumulated wisdom and faith-convictions into one beautiful volume is a great achievement. I cannot help feeling that this volume, *Mystics: The Beauty of Prayer*, is Craig's special legacy to all of us.

Though the work was published posthumously – thanks to the dedicated work of Neil Vaney and the New Zealand Marists, working with FitzBeck Publishing – it was pretty well intact and ready when Craig died in 2015. Indeed, it was a labour of love over the last decade of his life. He dreamed of writing something which would unpack the rich wisdom of a range of Christian spiritual writers using some favourite image, metaphor or symbol from their writings. It was constantly on his mind - as he worked away at other things he was constantly picking up material and ideas that would serve this purpose. The result is not only a beautiful anthology of teachings on the inner Christian life, serving to nourish the faith and spiritual journey of his readers, but a celebration of the importance of the image in transmitting a message. There was always something creative and imaginative in Craig's writing. In this book it seems to have found its proper idiom.

It is also a very practical book. As we find in the Introduction: "I have met Christians who have somehow silenced the murmur of music in their souls. Their Christian lives are a joyless burden, and they end their lives afraid of meeting the One to whom they gave their lives in faith. ... There are too many of these people in the world ... Fortunately, ... there have been countless others who have experienced God in another way ..." The author's intention is to offer something to all of us to discover a new and deeper freedom in our lives in God - a sustained invitation to live joyfully with the God who loves us.

I do not know why Craig chose the particular selection of spiritual writers presented in the book, apart from the fact that they spoke
very powerfully to him in his own life. Apparently it was the author's
intent to include other more recent writers and their favoured
images, but he ran out of time and energy. Perhaps he will inspire
someone else to continue the work....? What Craig has left us certainly provides a wide spectrum of samples from different traditions
representing over 2,000 years of Christian faith: from the Psalmist
to Caryll Houselander; from the Fathers of the early centuries to the
intense spiritual flowering of 16th Century Spain and 17th Century
France; from Medieval Europe to the heart of the Renaissance; from
East and West, men and women, religious and lay people, favourite
authors and lesser known geniuses.

For each one chosen Craig offers a most helpful and enlightening
introduction, situating the chosen author in his/her time and wider
context. He even manages to do this when the author is not known!
He concludes each chapter with a very helpful meditation on the
significance of the teaching conveyed through the image, sometimes
putting it in dialogue with an author from a different period, a different world, at other times, calling on his own wide experience of
living the spiritual life, and of accompanying people in their journey
of faith. In-between these two he simply presents the image, symbol
or metaphor the author has used to convey his meaning. Some of
these image-symbols are familiar: Julian's "nut", for instance, or the
butterfly of Teresa of Avila, and the reed of Caryll Houselander's
work the Reed of God; others are less obvious: Francis de Sales' "fall
in the ditch", the feather for Hildegarde and Cassian's "ploughman".
But all are beautifully elucidated in the text that follows. The struc-
ture of each section thus serves as a kind of frame around the central
work of art. It allows the chosen image to speak for itself to our
inner being, highlighted as it were by what surrounds it.

The result is a very rich encounter with many different people
and approaches to living a spiritual life. In a lovely lightness of
touch, the author is merely a facilitator of the encounter between
us and the image. Nothing is forced. We feel deeply respected and

freely engaged in this meeting of minds and hearts – free to take and leave what we want, to go at our own pace, to focus on that part that speaks to us at this time. We can take the figures presented in any order, as Craig himself does not seem to follow any logical, nor chronological ordering. The book behaves more like a poem than a manual – it leads us freely through a range of spiritual sensitivities and insights, allowing us to enjoy and rest and move on as we will. It is like someone showing you around his favourite garden: inviting you to engage with the different plants and flowers accordingly as they speak particularly to you at this particular time and in this particular place on life's pilgrimage.

I am very happy that Columba Press agreed to publish Craig Larkin's book. The two printings in New Zealand were quickly exhausted, but it was deemed too expensive a venture to try to market further printings wider afield. This new edition should enable a European-wide audience to access it. Columba are doing us all a great service.

Dear reader, I invite you to take this volume into your hands at a moment when you have some time and inner space to enjoy it, and engage in a dialogue with Christian wisdom that can only do you immense good. I have done so already, several times, and am ready to start anew!

PAUL WALSH, S.M.
Rome

INTRODUCTION

After living all my life as a professional Christian, my single and greatest disappointment with religion is that it has succeeded in making too many people afraid of God.

I have spent hours teaching, counselling, listening to and comforting people. Too many of them find their troubles rooted in fear of God. These are people who function well in a life full of responsibilities – as married people, as doctors, as teachers, as cooks or airline pilots – but who in their relationship with God are crippled by scruples and fears. Their religion is a matter of anxiety or bargaining, of calculation or attention to detail.

They are trapped in the externals of their faith. They suspect that these externals don't work any more, but they are afraid of breaking free of them in case some disaster might overtake them.

I've met ministers of religion who have become anxious functionaries of a religion that has not enabled them to be free. They are faithful gatekeepers of the church they serve, but they have not journeyed beyond the gate to see for themselves what is beyond; and sadly, they have prevented others from passing through the gate.

I've met Christians who have somehow silenced the murmur of music in their souls. Their Christian lives are a joyless burden, and they end their lives afraid of meeting the One to whom they gave their lives in faith.

There are too many of these people in the world.

Fortunately, throughout history there have been countless others who have experienced God in another way. These are the mystics who have experienced God as someone who has set them free and brought light to their lives. There's music in their soul, and their lives have been a song.

Whatever else they may have suffered in their lives, they looked on God as their lover, and they looked on themselves as God's lovers. These people wrote and spoke like the poets, the musicians, the artists of the spiritual life. Their writing was passionate, sensual, even at times erotic. In describing their experience of God, these lovers of God didn't use the straight lines of careful theology. Rather, they spoke in colours, in shapes, in music. They used images to describe their experience.

People like Augustine, Julian of Norwich, Teresa of Avila, John of the Cross, or Francis de Sales, described God as "a sea", or as "a fisherman". They wrote of life with God as "a journey" into "the desert", or "through a cloud" or "into a castle". They described the Christian as a "pilgrim" or a "journeyman". They likened prayer to "a game of chess". The one who searches for God needs to be like a "bird set loose" from the cord that attaches it to earth. And so on.

These cryptic and sometimes baffling symbols they left us were the only ways they could find to describe what the Lord was doing within each one of them. An early Christian writer, St Clement of Alexandria, put it this way: "Come, I will show you the Word and the mysteries of the Word, and I will give you understandings of them by means of images familiar to you." But like any lover, even when they had exhausted their images they confessed that they couldn't explain themselves properly, and in the end they could only say that "that's not really what I meant".

Because they wrote in the language of pictures and of passionate love, many were sometimes considered to be heretical, suspect or at the very least subject to correction in what they wrote. Many of the great mystics suffered misunderstanding and rejection because their language didn't fit into the framework of nuanced theology.

Gregory of Nyssa (335–394) was ignored for centuries by theologians, as was Jan Ruysbroeck (1293–1381). John of the Cross and Teresa of Avila both found themselves at odds with spiritual directors and experts in the spiritual life. The same was true of Henry Suso (1295–1366), John Tauler (1300–1361), Herry Herp (b.1478), Ignatius of Loyola (1491–1556), John Joseph Surin (1600–1665), and so on – even of St Thérèse of Lisieux and Thomas Merton. A constant cry of

Blessed Angela of Foligno when relating her own experiences was that her words would sound blasphemous.

In fact many of these lovers or friends of God suffered much more after their death at the hands of those who corrected their writings than they ever did during their lives at the hands of their enemies. In the end, the passage of time proved them to be more correct than their editors. And fortunately we are left with their rich images.

The compelling images used by these friends of God have one thing in common. They are about a God who has great desires for us; a Jesus who loves us and who wants us just to live in simple friendship with him and enjoy the journey of life with him. The psalmist talks with God as with a friend, berating God for abandoning him – "Why have you forgotten me? Why do I go about in mourning?"[1] – but also caressing God with words that lovers use – "My body pines for you".[2]

Why did Jesus "always teach in parables"? Because the spiritual life has its roots in the deepest, unconscious part of ourselves. We make contact with this life more by parables, by images and symbols than by literal language. And this is why travellers into the uncharted waters of the spiritual life can best and sometimes only speak in images.

Images release the music in the soul, and that's what Jesus meant when he said that he had come that we may have life, and have it in abundance. Life, and more life, and more life. This is what Jesus wants for us.

In his novel *Dr Zhivago*, Boris Pasternak puts these words on the lips of Nikolai Nikolaievich:

> "Let me tell you what I think. I think that if the beast who sleeps in man could be held down by threats – any kind of threats, whether of jail or retribution after death (by some transcendent God) – then the highest emblem of humanity would be the lion-tamer in the circus with his whip, not the prophet who sacrificed himself. But don't you see, this is just the point – what has for centuries raised man above the beast is not the cudgel but an inward music: the irresistible power of unarmed truth, the powerful attraction of its example. It has always been assumed that the most important things in the Gospels are the ethical maxims and commandments. But for me the most important thing is that Christ speaks in parables taken from life: that he explains the truth in terms of everyday reality."

"An inward music." That's what each one of us longs to hear and to sing. The music of God's song is not always joyful. Sometimes it is played in a minor key. But it is always music, and it is always "soulful"; and when the music stops, the inner life of the spirit begins to shrivel up and die.

I have chosen twenty images used by mystics – women and men – who lived at different times in the Church's history. I've lived for a long time with these images that they have left us. I've thought about them and looked at them from different angles. I've tried to analyse or explain them. In the end, the image remains and my words of explanation fall apart. But together these images sum up or express almost everything I know or have experienced of the spiritual journey. And taken individually, each image stands as a sort of landmark for anyone embarking on their own inner journey.

But since an image always contains more than is found in the literal meaning of the words, each image will evoke different levels of meaning for different people. This is why I advise you, the reader, to let the image speak for itself and say to you what you are meant to hear.

When Beethoven had played a new sonata for a friend, the friend asked him after the last note: "What does the music mean?" Beethoven returned to the piano, played the whole sonata again and said, "That's what it means!"

CRAIG LARKIN SM

Julian of Norwich

ulian of Norwich was a remarkable English woman who lived in Norwich in the fourteenth century.

That century was a chaotic time in European history, when medieval Christendom was coming to an end. Europe was torn apart by the Black Death, the 100 Years' War between England and France and the Peasants' Revolt. The Catholic Church was split by controversy: there were two and sometimes three popes each claiming the authority of the papacy, in Rome and in Avignon.

At the same time, this was an age when, in spite of all the confusion, chaos and disaster, there was a remarkable resurgence of religious spirit, particularly in England. Julian of Norwich belongs to a group of exceptional men and women – mystics in the English Church – who lived between 1250 and 1400.

Norwich lies to the east of the Midlands of England, 30 miles upstream from the coastal town of Yarmouth. Since it was a river city it became a strategic commercial centre, exporting wool out to Flanders and the Rhineland, and importing wine and lace into England. Norwich became a significant commercial centre, from which roads and waterways lead to London, Lincoln and York. In the fourteenth century it was the second largest city in England with a population of 6,000. The city was impressive. It had a cathedral with a soaring spire, a castle and above all a large number of churches.

In Julian's time there were approximately 60 churches in the city. There were monasteries and convents – 37 chapels, as well as cells for hermits in each of the 10 city gates.[3]

We know little about Julian. She has no known grave. There are no relics of her. Her writings were not discovered until 300 years after her death, and only published more widely 200 years after that. Until the 1970s she was almost unknown except to students of fourteenth century English language, who were fascinated by the fact that Julian was the first woman ever to write in English.

But we do know that she was born in 1342. She lived with her mother until about the age of thirty. She tells us that at some time in her early years she had asked three favours of God. The first was a "bodily sight" of the Passion of Christ, so she could share His suffering. The second was to have some form of suffering. And the third was to have three "wounds": the wound of true contrition, the wound of kind compassion and the wound of earnest longing for God.

Then on a dramatic day in 1373 – May 8th – she suffered a severe illness. Julian tells us that during her time of sickness everyone thought she was dying. Then the pain ceased and between four and nine o'clock in the morning she received fifteen "showings". Then she fell asleep and she had her last, her sixteenth "showing" of Jesus, divine and human, sitting enthroned in her heart. This last showing convinced her that "in us is he completely at home". A voice told her to treasure and ponder over all she had received.

From the age of 31 she lived as an anchoress in Norwich. Anchoresses were people who took vows to live a solitary life of prayer and meditation. They became significant in the towns. People would go to them for advice, consultation and a ready ear. A rule had been written for anchoresses, which laid down certain principles of life. If Julian had lived by this *"Ancrene Riwle"* her cell would have had three windows: one opening onto the church so she could hear Mass and receive Communion, another opening onto an inner room so that a servant could bring food and clean clothes and a third opening onto the roadway, so the anchoress could look out into the street and speak with people who sought advice.

Anchoresses were prey to two very human temptations: either to spend too little time listening to others, or to spend too much time listening to them. Aelred of Rivaulx, writing some 100 years after Julian, gives us a vivid description of some of the sorts of things that some anchoresses got up to:

> *"At her window will be seated some garrulous old gossip pouring idle tales into her ears, feeding her with scandal and gossip; describing in detail the face, appearance and mannerisms of now this priest, now that monk or clerk, describing too the frivolous behaviour of a young girl; the free and easy ways of a young widow who thinks what she likes is right, the cunning ways of a wife who cuckolds her husband while she gratifies her passions. The recluse all the while is dissolved in laughter, loud peals of laughter."* [4]

Mother Julian wrote her book only after twenty years of meditating on the experience of her revelations.

The most significant thing one can say of Julian's life, her style and her message is summed up in a word she uses frequently: "homely". She doesn't write of the usual subjects treated in mystical literature. She doesn't analyse or tell us how to eradicate the disorders in our lives. She doesn't mention the dark night of the soul or the mystical marriage with God. And she offers no techniques of prayer or contemplation. Everything she writes is "homely".

This makes her a wonderful guide in the spiritual journey. She reminds us to live in tranquility and peace with God. "Sin must needs be," she says, "but all will be well, and all manner of things shall be well." All will be well, Julian says, because all is love. "You know Our Lord's meaning in this thing? Know it well. Love was His meaning. Who showed it to you? Love. What did He show you? Love. Why did He show it? For love. Hold on to this and you will know and understand love more and more. But you will not know or learn anything else – ever!"

THE LITTLE NUT

*It was at this time that Our Lord showed me spiritually how
intimately He loves us. He showed me a little thing, the size of a
hazelnut, on the palm of my hand, round like a ball. I looked at
it thoughtfully and wondered, "What is this?" And the answer
came, "It is all that is made." I marveled that it continued to exist
and did not suddenly disintegrate; it was so small. And again
my mind supplied the answer, "It exists, both now and forever,
because God loves it."*

In short, everything owes its existence to the love of God.

*In this "little thing" I saw three truths.
The first is that God made it;
The second is that God loves it;
The third is that God sustains it.*

Julian of Norwich, *Revelations of Divine Love*

"He made us! He keeps us! He loves us!"

One of the first things we learn about the friends of God is that they were able to see God at work in everything, even the most ordinary and apparently insignificant things. What could be more homely than a little nut? And yet, what could be more profound than the insight that Julian gained and has left to us: "God made us. God keeps us. God loves us."

It's so easy, when we speak of the "love of God", to think that the important thing is our love for God. In fact, as Julian insists, the first and most important thing to believe in is God's love for us. The beginning of my journey into life in the Spirit comes when I realise and accept that God accepts me and loves me personally. The psalmist sang: "The Lord takes delight in his people." (Ps 149) God's love for me is not only a matter of accepting me, or putting up with me or forgiving me, but – like any parent with a new-born child – taking *delight* in this child.

Whenever I think of this mystery of God's unconditional love for us, the face of Christine comes to my memory. Christine was a natural, very attractive and fun-loving teenager with not a care in the world. Not until one tragic night some years ago. She had been at a party, and while driving home after the party, hit a power pole in her speeding car. Her girlfriend, who was a passenger, was killed. Christine survived because she was ejected through the windscreen on impact. I visited the hospital after the accident. My heart sank when I saw her. Her beautiful face was disfigured almost beyond recognition. I remember thinking, "O God, one drink too many, one split second of inattention, and this is the result." As the weeks passed, she began to realise that she would never be the person she was before. She watched as each visitor looked away from her face in shock and embarrassment.

But that wasn't the worst of it. Inside herself, that beautiful, self-confident, outgoing person began slowly to die. She became crippled with guilt for causing the death of her friend. "If onlys" raced compulsively through her mind. She lost her energy for living. I saw her slip deeper and deeper into depression and a sort of bitterness. She withdrew from life, and didn't want to see people or let them visit her. One exception was her boyfriend, who would come each day and sit by her bedside, saying little, just being there.

Ten years later I met Christine again. I couldn't believe the transformation. She still carried the awful scars of disfigurement on her face, but what an incredible inner beauty shone through those eyes! She proudly showed me her two children whom she obviously loved with great energy and tenderness. She had married her faithful boyfriend, and she made no bones about the fact that without his love and his belief in her, she would never have pulled through. Slowly and painfully, she had learned to accept that someone loved her for herself, in all her human pain, deformity and guilt. Here she was, a woman transformed by another's love, a woman who was able to let her inner beauty shine through her scars; who was able to love and energise others because she knew she was loved. Truly love is a fire that transforms!

Christine was fortunate. She found someone who accepted her, and through that experience she began to understand what it means to be accepted unconditionally by someone else. What happens to people who aren't so fortunate? Every human being craves – needs – to be accepted for what each one is. Nothing in human life has such a lasting effect as the devastating experience of not being accepted. A baby who is not welcomed is deprived from the start of its existence. A student who doesn't find acceptance doesn't learn. Many of the life stories of criminals reveal that somewhere in their history there was no one who really accepted them. When we feel unaccepted we compensate by all sorts of behaviours: boasting, bullying, rigid attitudes or behaviour, inferiority complexes, sexual compulsions, addictive drinking or gambling. These are all ways of scratching some form of acceptance from life. But each of these things leads to a dead end.

When we reflect on the lives of those friends of God and read of their incredible love and physical energy, we can't help asking: what was their secret? What explains the extraordinary energy of St Paul, whose evangelising journeys covered thousands of miles, who set up the Church in the Roman Empire – and all in the space of ten years! What explains the transformation of those Old Testament characters Isaiah (Is 43), or Jeremiah (Jer 1:5-8, 20:9-10), or Samuel (1 Sam 3:4)? What explains the transformation of a St John of the Cross, or a St Teresa or a St Ignatius of Loyola? Somehow, it was the conviction that they were loved and accepted in their scarred humanity, and loved unconditionally by a God "who takes delight in his people". "Loved sinners", they were transformed by the knowledge that God accepted and loved them. Somehow, they were all touched by the same insight of Julian: "God made me! God keeps me! God loves me!"

Our journey into the life of the Spirit begins with a call. Not a call in the first place to try to love God or to please God or to pacify God or to win merit in the sight of God, but rather an invitation to accept that before and beyond anything else, we have been accepted by a God who made us, who keeps us and who loves us. This truth belongs to the "ground of our being" and brings about an inner security.

Julian uses her "homely" style to describe this passionate love of God. She speaks of the Father and of Jesus as "our mother". "God is as really our mother as he is our father." Even more strikingly she says, "The human mother will suckle her child with her own milk, but our beloved mother Jesus feeds us with himself, and, with the most tender courtesy, does it by means of the holy sacrament." And as we mature in confidence and in prayer, our Lord treats us "like a wise mother, who changes her methods, but not her love".

Julian belongs to a long line of writers who have used feminine imagery in depicting God. In the psalms, God is portrayed as a midwife, who takes a child out of the womb and places it on its mother's breasts (Ps 21:10). God is depicted as a mother bird who protects her flock under her wings (Ps 35:8), or similarly as a nesting place where sparrows can find a home (Ps 83:4). In another psalm God is compared both to a master and a mistress (Ps 123:2). The book of Deuteronomy (Ch 32) and the Prophecy of Isaiah use maternal imagery in their descriptions of God's love. Isaiah is particularly rich in his descriptions of God as a mother crying out while giving birth, and offering her consoling breasts for the child to suck, comforting and nestling the child on her knees. And for me, the most beautiful image of God's maternal love is found in Isaiah, chapter 49: "Can a woman forget the child at her breast? Yet even if she could forget, I will never forget you." (Is 49:15)

In Christian spiritual writing, we find references to God as mother right back in the writings of the Fathers. Origen, Irenaeus, John Chrysostom, Ambrose and Augustine all use the image. Clement of Alexandria wrote,

> "And God himself is love; and out of love to us became feminine. In his ineffable essence he is Father; in his compassion to us he became Mother. The Father by loving became feminine; and the great proof of this is he whom he begot of himself; and fruit brought forth by love is love."

In Irenaeus there is reference to the "mother's breasts" of Christ, while Justin Martyr speaks of "the belly of Christ". Both Maximus the Confessor and Symeon the New Theologian speak of each Christian's vocation to give birth to Christ.

The Syriac tradition is particularly rich in feminine symbolism. This tradition sees the Holy Spirit as the feminine principle of God; and St Ephrem, the great composer of Christian hymns, uses maternal symbols in his compositions.

The twelfth century saw a strong resurgence of feminine imagery in spiritual writing. Mechtilde of Magdeburg made frequent use of feminine images. So also did mystics and saints such as Bernard of Clairvaux, Aelred of Rievaulx, Guerric of Igny, Isaac of Stella, William of St Thierry and especially Anselm of Canterbury.

It's within this developed tradition that we can place Julian of Norwich. In her *Revelations* we find images of motherhood: the womb, birthing, nurturing and caring. God is seen as a lover, a nurse, a teacher. "God is our Mother by nature and grace."

Four chapters of the *Revelations* (Chs 58 – 61) deal almost exclusively with this theme of maternity in God. Julian's reflections take the image of motherhood to a deep level. For her, God is not simply *like* a mother; God *is* all that a mother is. Julian stands in a long tradition of Christian experience which profoundly understands the maternal aspect of God's love.

But the tradition was not developed within mainstream Christianity, and for centuries this reflection on the maternal nature of God's love was put aside and given little attention. Only in recent times has this image received more respectful attention. This may partly explain why Julian was so often overlooked. In ages when the feminine was suppressed, her writings could well have been considered too extreme to be correct.

But Julian took the image of the motherhood of God to a startling conclusion. She believed that God, as any mother, will even use our sins to transform us. "Sin shall not be a shame to humans, but a glory ... The mark of sin shall be turned to honour."

Recognising our sinfulness or inner deformities is a humbling experience, but it gives us the opportunity to believe in the unconditional love of God and to entrust ourselves to that. We are damaged goods. Damaged – yes, but goods – certainly. "And this is what I made, what I keep and what I love," says God. "I can do great things with this!"

God's hope for all of us is to be what we were made to be, and to be wholly that. The struggle that this involves in each person is supported and made bearable by one thing: the conviction that we are reconciled, accepted and held in the grace of God. This helps us to accept ourselves as we are, and not live in the false world of pretence or make-believe. There's a delightful moment in the book *Zorba the Greek*, when Zorba says:

> *"The same thing's happening to you as happened to the crow."*
> *"What happened to the crow, Zorba?" "Well, you see, he used to walk respectably, properly, well, like a crow. But one day he got it into his head to try to strut about like a pigeon. But from that time on the poor fellow couldn't for the life of him recall his own way of walking. He was all mixed up, don't you see? He just hobbled about."* [6]

God doesn't want us to hobble about through life, trying to be something that we are not. God wants us to grow into the unique people we are supposed to be. The grace we are given is the grace of new life. This new life is, simply, new life – that is to say, a new world of possibilities, a new future which is to be welcomed day by day. We are called to grow.

John Tauler

 study of the history of Christian spirituality shows us that the Spirit's ways of working in individuals follow rules or laws quite beyond our human understanding or expectations. Historians have also drawn attention to another remarkable thing. Throughout the course of the last thousand years, through the action of the Spirit, particular currents of spiritual experience have moved more strongly in some parts of the world and in ways that one doesn't see in other parts.

In the thirteenth century for example, there was a remarkable flourishing of holiness in Italy. St Francis of Assisi, St Thomas Aquinas, St Bonaventure, Blessed Angela of Foligno and Jacapone da Todi all lived in thirteenth century Italy. And we could include here the poet Dante Alighieri.

In the latter part of the fourteenth century, a centre of mystical experience seemed to be located in England with people like Julian of Norwich, Richard Rolle, Walter Hilton and the author of *The Cloud of Unknowing.*

In the fifteenth century, we see a flourishing of mystical writings in the Netherlands, with Thomas à Kempis, author of *The Imitation of Christ*, Gerlach Peters and Hendrick Herp.

In the sixteenth century, Spain became a focal point of mystical experience. Ignatius of Loyola, Teresa of Avila, John of the Cross, Peter of Alcantara, Francis of Osuna, and Luis of Grenada lived in this century.

Into the seventeenth and eighteenth centuries similar movements occurred in France, with significant personalities like Francis de Sales, Jane Frances de Chantal, Pierre de Bérulle, and Jean-Pierre de Caussade.

In the latter part of the thirteenth century and the early part of the fourteenth century, almost like a link between the flourishing of mystical writing in thirteenth century Italy and fourteenth century England, there was a remarkable movement of spiritual writing in Germany. This Rhineland mysticism owes its origins to the Beguine mystic Mechthild of Magdeburg and was spearheaded by the Dominican Meister Eckhart and two other great Dominicans, Henry Suso and John Tauler.

Rhineland mysticism has often been contrasted with the Scholastic theology current in the Church at that time. In some aspects the contrast is notable. Theologians and mystics expressed themselves in current German rather than in Latin. There was more emphasis on preaching, with a preference for the New Testament and a strong emphasis on the person of Jesus. Lay people were seen as a vital part of the life and ministry of the Church.

John Tauler is one of the most important representatives of Rhineland mysticism. The son of prosperous parents, he was born in Strasbourg around 1300, and died 61 years later. He entered the Dominican Order at about the age of 15, attracted, he said later, by the ascetic life of the Order. His studies would have brought him into close contact with the great authors whom he frequently quotes: Augustine, Gregory, Bernard, Hugo and Richard of St Victor, Thomas Aquinas and Albert the Great.

From about 1339 to 1347 he lived at Basle, and it's here that he met Henry Suso. Tauler became involved in a large society called the Friends of God.

This movement involved men and women of all social classes and states of life: clerical, religious and lay. Members felt the need to draw together to cultivate a life of devotion and intense prayer in those times of social upheaval.

It is said that at the age of 40, John Tauler experienced a conversion which radically changed his life. One of his contemporaries described his preaching from this time on as capable of "setting the world aflame" because it was so full of compelling warmth and devotion.

Tauler was a disciple of Meister Eckhart whom he considered to be his master and teacher. At the same time, he was more practical and down-to-earth than Eckhart, and was able to transmit much of Eckhart's basic teachings when Eckhart was branded as heretical. Some of Eckhart's sermons were preserved under Tauler's name.

Tauler's special gift lies in his ability to bring the simple message of God's love to people at a time when they were prompted to think of their age as the time of the great Apocalypse, falling victim to superstitions and especially to fear – fear of God the Judge, fear of death, fear of hell. His sermons are written in concrete style with images and language that his listeners can understand. His message is about the simplicity of God and the gentleness of Christ.

The centre of Tauler's teaching is his belief that we can and should reach the experience of God through our ordinary daily work carried out in *love*. The eighty or so sermons he has left us show that he is very concerned to show that action in the world and the life of prayer form one unity and should not be separated. In one sermon he tells of a farmer who had been wrapped up in his everyday work. The man asked God whether he should stop his work and go to church. God, according to Tauler, said that the man should go on working for his bread by the sweat of his brow, in honour of the precious blood of Christ.

Tauler's teaching was subject to criticism in his own day and later. He seems to have suffered considerably during the last years of his preaching. One of his friends wrote to another friend: "Pray for our dear Father Tauler. He is generally in great distress because he teaches the truth as wholeheartedly as any teacher I know." During the sixteenth century the sermons of Tauler were condemned or forbidden in France, Spain and Belgium, and in the seventeenth century his teaching was aligned with the Quietist heresy, a stigma that remained until the nineteenth century.

It is clear that Tauler's preaching was not based on theory, but rather that it flowed from his own experience of life. In the end, Tauler leaves us with the impression that he is close to ordinary life.

THE FISHERMAN

The fisherman throws his fish-hook in order to take the fish, but he does not succeed unless the fish seize the hook. If the fish seize the bait, the fisherman is certain to take it and to draw it towards him.

Thus God has thrown into the whole universe and over all creatures beneath our feet, before our eyes and before our soul, his fish-hook, his bait, his net to draw us to him by means of all the things of this world.

He draws us by things pleasing, he leads us on by things which afflict us.

He who is not drawn has only himself to blame, for he has not bitten the bait which God has thrown him: he has refused to allow himself to be taken by his hook and in his net. Otherwise God would have certainly taken and drawn him to himself.

John Tauler, Sermon II for Holy Thursday

"By God I'm hooked!"

Many of us get stuck right at the beginning of our Christian lives. This is understandable. In many ways, our growth in the Christian life follows the pattern of our social development. In our social growth we all have to be taught ways of behaving in order to live as social beings, and often enough our deep-seated reluctance to change or to transcend ourselves can only be overcome by a certain degree of fear or by the promise of punishment or reward.

There are two in-built problems with this. The first is that our behaviours can easily become motivated by the need to please others. We learn to recognise who are the big people in our lives whom we need to please, and we learn how to avoid being caught out by those same big people. The second problem is that we run the risk of building an empty shell of our lives. Our external behaviours won't necessarily correspond to our inner dispositions.

It's probably inevitable that our first steps in Christian living might follow a similar pattern. Early on we pick up the impression that God is a "big person" whose anger needs to be avoided, or at the very least who needs to be pleased. Then we learn that certain things need to be done, or certain actions need to be performed in order to please God or to appease God's anger.

And so begins our journey along a path of a sort of "moralism" and in so doing we run the risk of building an empty shell of our lives. The gap between what we do or say and what we really believe gets wider and wider until a type of break-down takes place.

But we do get chances to break this cycle, even on the level of human behaviour. Take a young teenager who seems so incorrigible, who at home resists any efforts to be trained into the virtues of tolerance, patience, respect for others, altruism or even tidiness, who keeps parents awake at night wondering what state the car will be in when he or she returns home or what state he or she might be in. There comes a moment when this young person falls in love. Suddenly, almost overnight, things change. *Of course* she'll listen to another opinion, because the person she loves happens to hold it; *of course* he'll drive carefully, because he doesn't want her to be injured; *of course* they'll be respectful, because they don't want to hurt each other. Moral behaviour changes and even improves, but now for a different motive. It's not fear that drives their behaviours and conduct, but love.

There's an element here over which we have no control. We can't manufacture love. We can't make other people fall in love with us, and we can't make ourselves fall in love with others. It happens to us and within us. But on the other hand, love doesn't happen to us unless we're on the look-out for it. We'll never find the person of our dreams unless we put ourselves in the position where we might in fact stumble across that person.

In the spiritual life this process is contained in John Tauler's image of the fisherman. But from the start Tauler overturns a basic presumption that we have: that we are the ones who are searching for God. Tauler's image reminds us that it's not we who are searching for God; it's God who's on the look-out for us. We are not the angler hoping to catch God; it's God who is the angler patiently waiting to lure us with the bait of love and beauty.

Obvious as it may seem on paper, this is the one thing that most of us forget right at the start. We imagine God playing a sort of hide-and-seek game with us, teasing us and hiding from us, popping out at unexpected times and surprising us – or worse still, frightening us. This isn't the way God wants us to see things, and it isn't the experience of Tauler and other close friends of God.

Look at some of the famous characters in Scripture. Jeremiah cries out to the Lord: "You have seduced me, Lord, and I have let myself be seduced."(Jer 20:7) The prophet Hosea records the Lord saying: "I am going to lure you and lead you into the wilderness, and speak to your heart." (Hos 2:16). And think of that masterpiece of love poetry, the *Song of Songs*, which paints the picture of God as a lover running through the streets of a town in desperate search of his beloved – us. In his letter to the Philippians, St Paul writes: "I am still running, trying to capture the prize *for which Christ has captured me.*" (Phil 3:10)

We could go on, but there's no need to. The point that all the great friends of God make is that the first movement comes from God. God waits patiently, dangling the line of love in our direction, trying to capture our attention. We are invited to let God love us. When we have experienced this love, we are "hooked" on God.

I've come to realise how important this is. We belong to an age of analysis and definition, and we've done just that to our faith. We've discovered or invented words to describe a deep personal experience, and then we've analysed and defined those words almost out of existence. We've defined "faith" and "truth", "goodness" and "grace" and "mercy" in clear terms. The trouble with this, though, is that these realities then become things "out there", and beyond us. They lose their dynamic vibrancy and reality. Goodness and holiness, grace and mercy, become things that I strive for, or try to measure up to, or to gain, instead of being a wonderful process of being caught in love.

This is not what life in the Spirit is. Life in the Spirit is a matter of taking the bait put down for us and letting ourselves be drawn out of what we think is our normal existence into a different way of life.

This is what St Jerome tried to convey in a homily he gave to the newly-baptised Christians. He said:

> "You who have now put on Christ and follow our guidance are like little fish on the hook. You are being pulled up out of the deep waters of this world by the Word of God. And so you can say, 'In us nature is changed'. For fish which are taken out of the sea die; but the apostles have fished and taken us out of the sea of this world in such a way that we have been brought to life from the dead. When we were snatched from the waves we began to see the sun, we began to gaze upon the true light, and, troubled with excess of joy, we said to our souls, 'Hope in God, for I shall praise him, my Saviour and my God'."

I'm particularly fond of another image used by a medieval writer who speaks of God as a shrewd inn-keeper, who stands at the door of his drinking house, enticing people in by promises of good wine and food, and who quickly offers them a glass of good claret. Once they've tasted the wine, they're hooked, and the wily taverner has got them as customers. He fills them with his food and drink. He has done a good day's business. The medieval writer concludes:

"They drink all night, they drink all day;
And the more they drink, the more they may.
Such liking they have of that drink
That of none other wine they think,
But only for to drink their fill
And to have of this drink all their will.
And so they spend what they have, and then they sell or pawn their
coat, their hood and all they may, for to drink with liking while they
think it good." [8]

Jesus' parable of the treasure hidden in the field has much the same meaning. The French philosopher Paul Ricoeur sees the parable as an illustration of the way we gradually turn to God, and he sees this gradual movement taking place in three clearly defined stages. In the first, which he calls "the event", a man discovers a treasure. He stumbles on it by chance, as it were. But even though there's something of chance in his discovery, the lucky man only discovers it because he was already on the look-out for something. Then he goes home and sells his goods. It's a risky decision. He can't be absolutely sure the treasure is there under the soil, nor can he be sure what exactly the treasure is. But he knows that it's a treasure of some sort, and he takes the risk of selling everything he has. This second stage Ricoeur calls "the reversal". The man then takes the third step. He buys the field. Ricoeur calls this stage "the decision". It's a decisive step and one which radically changes his life.

The parable provides a good description of the process we call conversion of heart. But the parable leaves open another question which is crucial for the process of conversion. The unanswered question is: Who put the treasure there in the first place? And was the treasure really put there to be hidden, or was it put there in order to be found? Tauler reminds us in his image that the treasures that God has put in the field of this world are put there not to be hidden, but to be found.

This is where his image is rich. It puts the emphasis on God who drops the bait and who's waiting for us to take it. The kingdom of God is something that's hidden, but it's hidden in order to be discovered. It's something we must be ready to search for actively.

Tauler says that God's 'bait' is all around us in His creation. If we could only see! Often enough we ignore or don't notice the signs of God in creation. At other times we may be inclined to stop at creation, thinking that the beauty of creation itself is God. But God is beyond even the beauties of creation. The beauty of creation is the bait that draws us further into the depths to find God.

There's another aspect to Tauler's image. The fish are often to be found where the water is deep, and the deep is murky and dark; and it will often be in the deep, shadowy parts of ourselves that God the fisherman begins to 'hook us'. Many people discover with a liberating joy that God seemed to touch them and 'hook' them precisely in those areas that they considered were most dark, mysterious and even shameful.

Contemplating the image of the patient angler reminds us that a good angler knows that there are certain rules about fishing. Even fish are unique and can't all be treated in the same way. Some fish, even when they have taken the bait, need to be given a bit of play before they are finally caught. Some fish are cunning and seem to know what the angler is up to. The good fisherman knows that the moment for the final strike may take time and that some fish need to be tickled and coaxed into the net. John Bunyan, in his *Pilgrim's Progress*, puts it nicely:

> "You see the ways the fisherman doth take
> To catch the fish, what engines doth he make?
> Behold! How he engageth all his wits
> Also his snares, lines, angles, hooks and nets.
> Yet fish there be, that neither hook, nor line
> Nor snare, nor net, nor engine can make thine,
> They must be groped for, and be tickled, too,
> Or they will not be catched, whate'er you do." [9]

God the infinitely patient angler will go to any lengths to coax us into new life.

Augustine of Hippo

he very idea of a 'saint' is a problem for many of us. Often enough the word suggests remoteness, aloofness, a style of life alien from what we experience. Artists over the centuries have tended to increase the distance between 'saints' and 'us' with the way they have sometimes depicted these saints: eyes upwards, surrounded by an ethereal aura, ecstasy – or most often agony – etched onto their faces. They seem to make prayer and divine love a matter of the greatest suffering and sadness.

The story of Augustine blows away all these images. What sanctity he had was carved out of immense personal struggle, but was grounded in what we fear most – red-blooded passion. He is not a saint to depress us 'ordinary Christians' with his exceptional piety and his mystical experiences. In fact, he is unexceptional in many ways: in his sexual anxieties, in his complex relationship with his mother and his past, in the fickleness that led him to toy with various religious ideas as a young man, in his passionate need for friendship and peace of mind. Augustine knew what he was talking about when he wrote of desire. His whole life was a response to desire: a desire for intellectual acclaim and sensual satisfaction in his early life, and a desire for Truth and the love of God in his later life.

Augustine's path to God followed the way of struggle to emerge from intellectual error and moral disorder. In this he had to cope with all the tricks we ourselves are so familiar with: evasion, rationalisation, fear of letting go, putting off the moment of truth. His message is that out of failure a life of spiritual freedom can be born, and the unexpected stuff of humanity can provide the ground for beauty and truth. It is because of his similarity to us, and not only because of his saintliness, that we can confidently look on him as a guide on our journey.

Augustine was born at Thagaste in North Africa, of a pagan father and a Christian mother, Monica. Monica was a remarkable woman, one of the most powerful, possessive, yet deeply spiritual mothers in the history of Christendom. Monica's Christianity was simple, direct and full of faith – so different to the complex mixture of intellectual pride and self-doubt that tormented her brilliant son for so many years.

Augustine received a Christian education, and then went to Carthage where he studied rhetoric. Then he abandoned Christianity, joined the Manichaean sect, and took a mistress to whom he remained faithful for 15 years, and by whom he had a son whom they named Adeodatus (gift from God). In 383 he left Carthage for Rome, and at about the same time he became disillusioned with Manichaeism. He went north to Milan, became drawn to the famous St Ambrose, and gradually, after a tortuous journey, became a Catholic and was baptised on Easter Eve, 387.

The story of Augustine's conversion is recounted in his famous autobiographical book, *Confessions*. It is one of the most remarkable autobiographies in the world. Augustine uses the word "Confessions" in the sense of a statement of truth, a statement of praise. Certainly, through the book he confesses his disordered life and his misdeeds, but he does so in praise of the God who had called him, and who is the beginning and the end of all human desires.

The *Confessions* are the navigation points of a journey of desire, the story of a man's capacity for God being stretched further and further, till at last he allowed God to take over. For this strong, virile soul, who in his own words was "in love with love", the journey to God was through a purification of love, a stretching of desire. There is a great contrast between his early confession:

"*What was there to bring me delight*
except to love and be loved?
I was not yet in love, but I was in love
with love;
I sought for something to love, for I was
in love with love.
To love and to be loved was sweet to me,
and all the more if I enjoyed my loved
one's body."

and his later entry, after having taken his leap of faith and love:

"*You are my God, and I sigh for you*
day and night!
Too late have I loved you, O beauty
so ancient and so new ...
I tasted and I hunger and thirst for you.
You touched me, and I burned for
your embrace!"

There are definite key moments in Augustine's journey to God. First, there is his first experience or taste of God. Then follows the beginning of his struggle with himself. The third key moment is his struggle to overcome his reluctance to let God take over. Finally, there is the decision, the YES, at which "I needed nothing more. Instantly, as if before peaceful light streaming into my heart, all the dark shadows of doubt fled away". The tone of the *Confessions* changes to one of tranquility and peace. Augustine's famous phrase from this book of his Confessions sums up his life: "You have made us for yourself, O God; and our hearts are restless till they rest in you." Augustine was finally "hooked on Love".

Augustine defined our human nature as *capax dei* – capable of receiving God. Human though we are, we can be stretched to contain God. Human nature needs to be stretched – it wants to be stretched – and its whole purpose is to be stretched. It all depends on which way we want to be stretched. The decision is which direction to point our noses.

This truth isn't so easy. We are familiar with and perhaps identify with Augustine's famous prayer to God as he struggled within himself: "Give me chastity – but not yet!" Whether it's chastity, or the Spirit, or new life, the only thing more uncomfortable than the state we are in is the fear that God may actually give us what we ask for!

The turning point for Augustine was when he faced the desire beyond his desires. Then he took the bait.

THE STRETCHED BAG

The whole life of a Good Christian is a holy desire.

Suppose you want to fill some sort of bag, and you know the bulk of what you will be given, you stretch the bag or the sack of the skin or whatever it is. You know how big is the object that you want to put in it, and you see that the bag is narrow, so you increase its capacity by stretching it. In the same way by delaying the fulfillment of desire God stretches it, by making us desire He expands the soul, and by this expansion He increases its capacity.

Then, brothers and sisters, let us desire because we are to be fulfilled.

Look at St Paul stretching wide his heart to make it big enough to receive what was to come. He says, in effect, "Not that I have already obtained this or am already perfect; brethren I do not consider that I have made it my own."

This is our life, to be exercised by desire. But we are exercised by holy desire only in so far as we have cut off our longings from the love of the world. I have already pointed out – empty that which is to be filled. You are to be filled with good: pour out the bad.

St Augustine, *Treatise on the first letter of St Johnw*

I HAVE A DREAM!

Watching any TV game-show, or making a visit to any gym or weight loss programme makes one realise how much of our lives are propelled by desire. Desire for money, or fame, or beauty, or health, or fitness or knowledge – whatever it is, desire of some sort will usually be somewhere at the centre of our lives.

Now there's everything right about desires. Desires give us energy. Even a wrongly-aimed desire can be realigned, but a life without desire is no life at all.

In his instructions to someone learning to pray, St Ignatius of Loyola suggests that the person should begin each period of prayer focusing on one issue: *id quod volo* – what I want. And at the end of the time of prayer, he or she is encouraged to reflect: "Did I get what I want?" It's a simple technique, and perhaps surprising as an instruction for prayer, but it underlines the fact that we don't get anything that we think is valuable unless we actually want it. If we don't want *some*thing, we'll end up getting *no*thing.

The journey to God begins with desire but with this difference: the desire that draws us is not the desire for something outside of ourselves. It's not some 'thing' to be acquired. It's the desire that God, working within us, will stretch and expand us as breath expands and stretches a balloon. Augustine's image of the stretched bag or the balloon describes it exactly.

Holiness means allowing the Spirit of God within me to expand me beyond my own limits. This was the great realisation that St Paul came to in his conversion. Before and after his conversion, St Paul was the same person temperamentally. He was just as passionate after his experience on the road to Damascus as he was before. The change came about in the direction of his desire. Before his conversion he passionately desired the death of the followers of Jesus. After his conversion he desired with the same passion that they come to life in the Spirit. In one of his letters, he wrote: "Glory be to

God, whose power working in us can do infinitely more than we can hope for or even imagine." (Eph. 3:20) Paul understood that God is a powerful force within us, like a mighty breath, trying to expand our self-imposed limits, trying to extend our capacity for love, for goodness, for joy.

So there are two sides to this coin. On one side is the question: "What is it that I desire?" But on the reverse side is the other question: "What does God desire for me?" God does have desires for us, and our task is to make sure that what we desire is what God desires for us.

God has a dream for us, and we can find out a lot about that from the Scriptures. God hopes:

- that I will believe that God loves me madly, that I will let God seduce me and love me (Lam 3:22, Song of Songs 2: 10–14, Hosea 2:16, Isaiah 43, 49)
- that I will be able to call God "Abba – Daddy" (Jer 3:19, Hosea 11:1–4, Gal 4:6)
- that I will have life, and more life, and more life (John 10:10)
- that I will be able to let go and be free (John 8:36)
- that I will be filled with the breath of God's spirit so that my hidden self may grow strong (Eph 3:16)
- that I will know the love of God and be filled with God's utter fullness (Eph 3:19)
- that my life will be full of thanksgiving (Col 2:6).

If only we could desire what God desires for us! But that's not so easy because it means being stretched beyond our own limits.

A teacher in a small-town school spotted a pupil with talent. After coaching him through his secondary education, he said to the student: "If I were you, I'd take the chance to go to college. There won't be much else I could teach you around here. You would stay the same age all your life." [10]

Sadly, we've all come across people who've stayed the same age all their lives. Perhaps life presented them with tougher problems than they could solve. Or perhaps they received a major blow to their self-esteem and self-confidence that left them "stuck" at a moment of their growth. These are people whose happiness was arrested at a certain moment in their lives; whose reference point was a particular time when life seemed to be idyllic. They can find satisfaction only by endlessly repeating stories of some past time, which probably never existed anyway.

I saw a news report that told of a man who for some reason stopped growing physically. The headlines spoke of "an adult trapped inside a baby's body." The man is 40 years old, but his body has grown only to the age of 10. It's a rare case of delayed physical growth.

Arrested emotional and spiritual growth is a lot more common.

Over many years I've had the great privilege of watching people 'rise to the bait' of God's love, or I've seen them stretched and expanded by the Spirit. But I've come across cases of arrested spiritual growth. I've met people who have stayed the same age for most of their adult lives, and have never realised the spiritual potential that's in them. I've met and lived with people who still nursed injuries, real or imagined, that they received sometimes 40 years previously. Their inner clocks have stopped. The energy that could have been devoted to life, to love, to service of others, to prayer and growth in the Spirit, has been frustrated and blocked.

We have within ourselves more resources of energy than have ever been tapped, more talent than has ever been exploited, more strength than has ever been tested, more joy than we could ever use for ourselves, more to give than we have ever given.

And God's plan for us is much greater than we could imagine. It's certainly not to stay the same size and the same age inside all our lives.

Macarius, one of the Desert Fathers, uses the image of a newborn baby to describe how growth occurs after baptism. The baby is complete at birth. It possesses everything, he says; every limb, organ, muscle and bone it will ever have. Yet now comes the moment for growth. And it grows by stretching.

How does one move from the state of what T.S. Eliot so aptly calls "living and partly living" to that state of freedom and fullness in the life of the spirit? The link is desire.

St Thomas Aquinas says that desire is the faculty which receives, so that the bigger our desire is, the more we can receive. This is exactly what Augustine means by his image of the bag that's stretched.

All too easily we think that our desires are to be curbed, that somehow growth towards God means suppressing our red-blooded drives. Often enough we fear those two red-blooded passions of anger and sexuality, thinking that they must somehow be eliminated. But these two appetites are just manifestations of two very important qualities: energy and love. They need to be directed, not suppressed. To suppress the drive is to suppress the force of life. A life without these two drives is no life at all. It's the life of a balloon that hasn't been blown up.

Psychologists are right in reminding us of the two-fold role of anger in our lives. Directed the right way it moves us to go beyond ourselves, to overcome our limitations, to stretch ourselves, to overcome obstacles, to become heroes or mystics. Directed the wrong way it leads us to become vandals and mischief-makers.

The same can be said for our sexual desires. Directed the right way they bring us in touch with our longings and celebrations and delights, and they help us to enter into the longing of God. To split sexuality off into the realm of the non-spiritual is simultaneously to deny it some of its deepest meaning and to deprive ourselves of a significant source of spiritual growth.

We may try to deny that we have these drives within us, but if we do we'll consign ourselves only to dullness and to death. Frankly, we'll become boring. And the more we try to tame ourselves or reduce our desires and hopes, the less we become what God wants us to be.

In a beautiful section in one of his homilies, John Chrysostom comments on a passage in St Paul's Second Letter to the Corinthians. He says: "Just as what brings heat makes things expand, so it is the gift of love to stretch hearts wide open. It is a warm and glowing virtue." Then Chrysostom writes: "For he who is loved wanders in the inmost heart of the lover without any fear." [11]

I love his description of the trust that comes with deep love: to be able to wander in the inmost heart of the beloved without any fear. This is what Jesus wants of us. "Make your home in me as I make my home in you." He wants us to be able to wander round in his inmost heart, finding infinite space and many little corners to rest in. He wants us to feel at home with him. And at the same time he wants to be able to wander in our inmost heart – expanding it as he does. The work of asceticism, the struggle of self-denial is not the work of breaking down walls so that God can enter in. It's the work of allowing God who is already within us to push our walls gently but firmly outwards, making room for the infinite. "Blessed is the person whose desire for God has become like a lover's passion for the beloved," wrote John Climacus in the seventh century. [12]

What we and the saints have in common is passion and desire. So what's the difference between them and us? Why are our desires and wants exhausted without being satisfied while theirs seem to be fulfilled? It's because we limit the scope of our desires to what we think already satisfies us, or we fear to take the risk of reaching out for "the more" that we look for in those small moments of ecstasy we enjoy in music or art or sex. These experiences beckon us, stir up in us the longing for something infinite, but they don't satisfy it. They may exhaust our desires, but they can't fulfil them.

Augustine has a very down-to-earth description of this inner strug-gle to expand our inner selves when he speaks of his efforts to let his sexual desires open him out to God. He wrote in his *Confessions*:

> "*I was like someone who is just waking up, but still overcome by deep drowsiness, sinks back again... 'Right away. Yes, right away. Let me be for a little while.' But 'right away' was never right now, and 'let me be for a little while' stretched out for a long time ... for I feared that you would hear me quickly and would heal me of my lust which I wished to have satisfied rather than extinguished.*"

When this invitation to expand our horizons comes to us, we have two options: either we listen to the voice of fear which whispers to us that it's too difficult, or too extreme, or too silly to take the risk; or we listen to the voice of risk which tells us to make room inside ourselves and let our walls and barriers be stretched from the inside. Look again at Augustine's image. At the end, he has a significant re-mark: "I have already pointed out – empty that which is to be filled!"

There's a lot to be said for emptying our inner house of some of the junk that's there.

Origen of Alexandria

icture this. A young boy of 15, during the persecutions of Christians in the second century AD, sees his father being dragged off for execution for being a Christian. The ardent young man, passionately committed to the Risen Jesus, wants to run off with his father and win the prize of martyrdom by announcing himself as a Christian. He is dissuaded only by a ruse of his mother, who hides his clothes so that he can't leave the house.

The young boy, Origen, made up for this by writing an earnest letter to his father exhorting him to face death, and cautioning him "not to change your mind because of us". This letter undoubtedly became the basis for a treatise that Origen wrote later in his life entitled *Exhortation to Martyrdom*.

Origen's thirst for martyrdom came from his passionate temperament and his religious fervour which showed itself in an extreme form of asceticism. This in its turn probably explains an aspect of Origen's life which fascinates his biographers, namely his literal interpretation of the words of Jesus about people who made themselves eunuchs for the sake of the Kingdom. In his desire to take the words of the Gospel seriously Origen attempted to castrate himself. Later in life he thought better of such an extreme gesture and he wrote disparagingly of those who interpreted the Scriptures too literally.

Compared to other early Christian writers, we have a great deal of information about Origen. Although he himself left very few personal details in his own writings, he had an enthusiastic admirer in the historian Eusebius of Caesarea. In his book on the history of the Church, Eusebius devotes all of Book VI to the life of Origen.

The eldest of seven children, Origen was born in 184 or 185 in Alexandria, Egypt. Alexandria was a centre of commerce and culture, and it was the birthplace of Neoplatonism, a philosophical approach which profoundly influenced Origen's thinking and writing.

Origen was one of the first truly philosophical thinkers not only to refute pagan and Gnostic ideas, but also to offer an alternative system that was credible. He was also the first systematic commentator on the Greek Bible. He commented on most of the Old Testament, on all the Gospels except the Gospel of St Mark, and on most of the Epistles of St Paul.

At the age of 18 he was put in charge of what came to be known as the Alexandrian Catechetical School. This 'school' was not an official establishment, but a loosely-bound group of people whose aim was to explore and explain the Christian belief, and to prepare converts for baptism. But under the leadership of Clement of Alexandria and later of Origen, the 'school' became a major influence in the early Church, especially in its attempts to put the Christian faith into an intellectual context. The school was characterised by its attempts to look below the literal interpretation of Scripture to find the allegorical meaning of the words and events recorded in the Bible. Origen's prolific writings contributed greatly to the thrust of this catechetical school.

His spiritual vision can't be separated from the Neoplatonic philosophy which underpinned his thinking. In Plato's view, the human soul, before being incarnated in a body, had already existed in a previous time. The end of the soul's journey is to arrive at a state that it enjoyed previously. The soul ascends to the divine by detaching itself from earth, passing through the love of beautiful physical objects, to love of beautiful actions and then to love of absolute beauty. Contemplation of beauty is the most perfect life for any human.

Origen takes this framework and develops a Christian spirituality within it. He too describes three stages in the soul's journey to God.

First, there is the stage of detachment, in which the Christian wakes himself from the state of forgetfulness of God. Then there is the stage of struggle or asceticism, in which the Christian attempts to lose surplus spiritual weight, trims up and becomes spiritually fit. Finally there is the stage of "participation in the *Logos*" or attachment to the eternal Jesus in heaven.

His two most significant spiritual works were his *Exhortation to Martyrdom* and his treatise *On Prayer*.

Origen was one of the most profound spiritual writers of the early Church. His thinking influenced all Christian spirituality, especially, but not only, in the East. He had a brilliant mind, and was a man of intense spirituality. But despite this, he has always been kept at arm's length by theologians over the centuries.

Some of his conclusions and reflections in his chief work *On First Principles* led theologians to question his orthodoxy. In fact the Second Council of Constantinople in 553, 300 years after his death, condemned him as a heretic.

Though many of his teachings were condemned, his influence has never been lost. He had a significant influence on monasticism in the East, and his teaching influenced the writings of Evagrius of Pontus, Gregory of Nyssa, Dionysius the Areopagite and Maximus the Confessor as well as the humanist writers into the nineteenth century.

Origen began and ended his life in times of violent persecution. His youthful dream to die for the Lord was fulfilled when at the age of 69, during the persecutions of the Emperor Decius, he was put in prison and subjected to prolonged torture. We are told that his judges took care not to kill him, as the apostasy of such a great Christian leader would be more valuable to the anti-Christian cause than his martyrdom. Eusebius tells us that Origen endured chains, darkness, threats of fire and having his legs "pulled four paces apart in the torturer's stocks." But Origen, who had spent much of his life exhorting others to martyrdom, did not crumble. Though he lived for some time after the persecution, from early times he was considered to be a virtual martyr as a result of his torture.

THE HIDDEN SPRING

Each one of our souls contains a well of living water. It has in it...
a buried image of God. It is this well... that the hostile powers have
blocked up with earth. But now that our Isaac (Christ) has come, let
us welcome his coming and dig out our wells, clearing the earth from
them, cleansing them from all defilement... We shall find living water
in them, the water of which the Lord says, "He who believes in me,
out of his heart shall flow rivers of living water." (John 7:38)

For he is present there, the Word of God, and his work is to
remove the earth from the soul of each one of you, to let your
spring flow freely. This spring is in you and does not come from
outside because "the kingdom of God is in the midst of you".
(Luke 17:21) It was not outside but in her house that the woman
who had lost her silver coin found it again. (Luke 15:8) She had
lighted the lamp and swept out the house, and it was there that
she found her silver coin. For your part, if you light your "lamp",
if you make use of the illumination of the Holy Spirit, if you "see
light in his light", you will find the silver coin in you. For the
image of the heavenly king is in you. When God made human
beings at the beginning, he made them "in his own image and
likeness". (Genesis 1:26) And he does not imprint his image on the
outside but within them. It could not be seen in you as long as your
house was dirty, full of refuse and rubbish... but, rid by the Word
of God of that great pile of earth that was weighing you down, let
the "image of the heavenly" shine out in you now... The maker of
this image is the Son of God. He is a craftsman of such surpassing
skill that his image may indeed be obscured by neglect, but never
destroyed by evil. The image of God remains in you always.

Origen, *Homily on Genesis 1,4*

"Christian, acknowledge your dignity!"

Two young parents, proudly presenting their new-born baby for baptism, are often surprised and even shocked at some of the prayers surrounding the ceremony of the baptism, which refer to the power of satan, to exorcisms, and to original sin. "How could anyone associate sin with this helpless, trusting, open and totally loveable little bundle of innocence?" they ask. Yet, within a short time they are equally surprised and shocked to realise that this same child can show signs of naughtiness, self-will and downright bad behaviour. "Where did our baby pick up this?" they ask, amazed that despite the loving and caring environment they had provided, somehow this little bundle of innocence is not quite so innocent after all.

In the Book of Genesis, the story of Adam and Eve and the Garden of Eden is an attempt to explain the mystery of darkness in the human heart. The story is an allegory, and it tries to explain what we are all conscious of: something has gone wrong somewhere in our human story. We all know how much we desire goodness and love. Why is it so difficult, then, to be good? How do we explain this desire to be good and an equal tendency to do harm to ourselves and others?

The Fathers of the Church, especially the Fathers of the Eastern Church, had a way of reflecting on this human paradox. They began their reflection with the words from the first chapter in the Book of Genesis which describe humans as being made "in the image and likeness of God." [13] They expanded this in a phrase that was first coined by St Athanasius and repeated by others after him: "God became human that in him humans might become God." [14] Before we too quickly dismiss that statement as exaggeration, let's reflect on what the Fathers of the Church meant. What Athanasius is saying was put succinctly some centuries later by William of Saint-Thierry who said that we do not become God, but we become *"what God is"* (*quod Deus est*).[15] As humans, we are able to share in the qualities of God. Our existence, our intelligence, our loving, our joy and ultimately our eternity are a share in these qualities of God. St. Basil of

Caesarea writes, "The human being is an animal who has received the vocation to become God." [16] Origen put it another way: "Every spiritual being is, by nature, a temple of God, created to receive into itself the glory of God." [17]

In commenting on the statement found in the creation story in the Book of Genesis, the Fathers make a distinction between the two words, "image" and "likeness". They say that by the very fact that we are created we bear the image of God, and this image of God can never be lost. The likeness of God, on the other hand, our greater resemblance to God, can be lost by sin and can be regained by the practice of virtue.

Gregory of Nazianzen describes God as an architect who in creating humans, creates a new universe that's both visible and invisible, and contains contradictory elements:

> *"God created a being at once earthly and heavenly, insecure and immortal, visible and invisible, halfway between greatness and nothingness, flesh and spirit at the same time ... an animal en route to another native land, and, most mysterious of all, made to resemble God."* [18]

Gregory's phrase is striking: human beings are "halfway between greatness and nothingness ... and made to resemble God". This is why the Fathers put so much stress on the dignity of the body, and the dignity of human nature as such. They didn't spend much time in arguments about the immortality of the soul. But they spent a lot of time arguing about the resurrection of the body. The human being is not a soul trapped inside a body, waiting for liberation from this prison of flesh, as some philosophers had argued. The body, and the human person, is made in the image of God, and as Origen says in his explanation of the image of the pile of earth: "The image of God remains in you always."

But while the image of God in us can never be lost, our likeness to God can be lost –and it can be regained. It is lost by sin and it can be restored in us by the grace of the Holy Spirit, found in and through the life of the Church. Origen's description of the lump of earth may not be very poetic, but it is effective. The image of God in us is like a beautiful and fresh subterranean spring that's *there*, that flows under the surface of every human being, and that struggles to come to the surface and flow into the vast lake or sea of God's presence. Our sins, our mischievousness, our willful self-concern act like clods of earth that block the spring's path.

The effort to clear the blockage is what we do, by the power of Jesus and the Spirit. This effort is what the Fathers called *askesis*. *Askesis*, from which we get the word asceticism, is simply the human effort that we exert to remove what blocks the inner spring that's bubbling up in the "fathomless depth" of our being. We don't engage in this struggle just for the sake of it, and even less because we think our body or our human nature needs to be treated harshly. Our struggle, our askesis, our asceticism, our discipline, is aimed at one noble goal: to release the beautiful spring that's inside us.

Gregory of Nyssa, in one of his homilies, says:

> "When God created you he enclosed in you the image of his perfection, as the mark of a seal is impressed on wax. But your straying has obscured God's image ... You are like a metal coin: on the whetstone the rust disappears. The coin was dirty, but now it reflects the brightness of the sun and shines in its turn. Like the coin, the inward part of the personality, called the heart by our Master, once rid of the rust that hid its beauty, will rediscover the first likeness and be real ... So when people look at themselves they will see in themselves the One they are seeking." [19]

This wonderfully positive view of human nature is what motivated so many of the Fathers of the Church to remind Christians of their high vocation. In another homily, Gregory of Nyssa says:

> "The sky is not an image of God, nor is the moon, nor the sun, nor the beauty of the stars, nor anything of what can be seen in creation. You alone have been made in the image of God ... There is nothing so great among beings that it can be compared with your greatness." [20]

It's no wonder that St Leo the Great's Christmas sermon in Rome exhorted the people: "Christian, acknowledge your dignity!" [21]

I would really love Christians who take up the Christian journey (beginning with myself) to start with this view of our human nature, our bodies and our vocation as human beings. And yet it has to be admitted that for many of us these statements from the Fathers of the undivided Church ring strangely and seem scarcely credible. At least, they hardly influence our day-to-day behaviours.

The reason for this goes back to a debate in the fourth and fifth century of the Church's history between St Augustine and the British theologian Pelagius. Pelagius proposed the theory that human souls, being created by a good God, were by definition good. He claimed that we didn't inherit sin or guilt from our first parents. If we sin, it is because we choose to; and similarly, if by an act of supreme effort we decide to do good, then we can do so. Augustine was adamantly opposed to this understanding of Pelagius' teaching. From his personal experience, Augustine understood what St Paul meant when he wrote:

> *"Though the will to do what is good is in me, the performance is not ... every single time I want to do good it is something evil that comes to hand..."* [22]

Augustine's conclusion was based on Paul's words in the same letter: "Sin entered the world through one man, and through sin death, and thus death has spread through the whole human race..." [23] For Augustine, not only did we inherit the sin of Adam and Eve, but in ourselves we are a lump of sin. If we do good, it is by the grace of God, not by our own efforts.

The debate between the followers of Augustine and those of Pelagius became one of the most significant debates of the early Church, and the debate still continues in different ways. The difficulty with debates is that words are often imprecise, and often divide people. People take stands that are mutually exclusive; opponents demonise each other and people search for which side is 'right' and which side is 'wrong' with nothing in the middle. In the debate about grace and free will Augustine was declared the winner, and Pelagius the loser. But while Pelagius was wrong, he wasn't totally wrong; and while Augustine was right, he wasn't totally right. Augustine's view can easily lead us to forget that great truth, stressed by the early Fathers of the Church, that we are made in the image of God.

On the other hand, Origen's reflection on our human dignity as images of God led him to pose another question. If we are made in God's image, and if this image can never be lost, and if God desperately wants us all to be caught up in happiness forever, then how can we talk of everlasting damnation and hell? If all things are to be summed up in Christ at the last day when "God will be all in all",

[24] then things will be at the end as they were at the beginning of creation. Origen proposed that all of creation, all human beings, and even the demons, will eventually be saved, even if it takes innumerable ages to do so. He believed that the human intellect – being in the image of God – would never freely choose oblivion over closeness to God; and that in the end God's powerful love will soften even the hardest heart.

Even though it was officially condemned, Origen's teaching has never quite gone away. It is evident in the writings of some of the Fathers of the Church of the East, and it is still a strand in some aspects of Russian spirituality.

These are weighty arguments. Right now my efforts and energies are spent in believing that I'm made in God's image, which cannot be lost, and that God is a mad lover, madder than we could ever be, and keener for us to be saved than we are ourselves. About hell, we need to believe that our free will gives us the capacity to choose even to reject God. But we need also to believe that Christ's love is stronger than death and deeper even than hell. I'm happy to leave those other matters for God to work out, but I'm inclined to join the greats of the East – Origen, Gregory of Nyssa, Maximus the Confessor, Isaac of Nineveh and others – who leave the door open for all to be saved in the end.

I like to remember that wonderful story from the Desert Fathers about Antony who was thinking about the big questions: why some good people die young and some bad people live long and well; why some people are poor and some are rich; who gets to heaven in the end and who goes to hell. Antony heard the voice of God telling him to mind his own business: "Antony, keep your attention on yourself; these things are according to the judgment of God, and it's not to your advantage to know anything about them'.' [25]

Good advice.

Pseudo-Macarius

n our days of strict rules regarding copying of another person's text, it may come as a surprise to know that at an earlier moment in history plagiarism was not at all uncommon. It fact, it was not uncommon for a writer not only to take over another's text and call it his own, but even to take over an author's name!

There could have been several reasons for this. Sometimes an unknown writer assumed the name of a more famous person in order to give the writer a certain authority. This happened, for example, in the late fifth century when a Syrian writer assumed the name Dionysius the Areopagite. By taking the name of the companion of St Paul, this author gave greater credibility to his own writings. Scholars today refer to him as the "Pseudo-Dionysius". Or it sometimes happened that a writer whose reputation was suspect assumed or was given the name of another person so as to free his writings from criticism or condemnation. This happened, for example, when Origen's writings were condemned by the Second Council of Constantinople in 553. The writings of the great spiritual master Evagrius of Pontus, who was a disciple of Origen, were condemned also. But monks who didn't want Evagrius' teachings to be lost published them under the name of Nilus of Sinai, and for centuries Evagrius' text was thought to have been written by this author Nilus. It could also happen that a writer might write in the style of some well-known author, and then assume the author's name to indicate that even though the author named had not actually written the text, he would have, if he had thought of it!

So it happened that in the late fourth and early fifth century, a Syrian writer placed his writings under the name of Macarius, who was one of the great Fathers of the Egyptian Desert of the fourth century. This author wrote 'in the style' of Macarius, and for a long time he was assumed by scholars to have been the famous St Macarius of the Egyptian Desert.

But who were these Desert Fathers – and Mothers, for there were such – and what was the reason for the phenomenon we call the Desert period in Christian history?

The phenomenon dates back to the fourth and fifth centuries, which was an incredible period of time in the history of the Church. These centuries produced characters such as St Jerome, St Augustine, St Ambrose, St John Chrysostom, St Athanasius, and the great Cappadocian Fathers Basil, Gregory of Nyssa and Gregory Nazianzen. The fourth century also saw the beginnings of the breakdown of the Roman Empire and the shift of the capital of the Empire from Rome to Constantinople. And it saw an amazing movement of men and women into the desert areas of Egypt, Syria, Palestine and Arabia. From this time we date the beginning of Christian monastic life in three different forms: hermit life, community life and something midway between the two.

As the Roman Empire began to crumble from within and without, these men and women went into the desert areas for three chief reasons: to escape the shipwreck of the world around them; to fight with the demons both inside themselves and in the deserted caves where it was believed that they lived; and through that struggle to discover God. In this way they believed that they would find 'salvation'.

The desert waste-lands of Egypt or Syria were a symbol of the much more dangerous territory known as the human heart. So these desert dwellers not only entered the wilderness of a geographical desert, but through their struggles they mapped the wilderness of the human heart. They learned what tricks we humans play on ourselves, what prevents us from opening up to others, what resistances we use against the difficult but liberating task of discovering our true selves. Well before the science of psychology was recognised, these masters of the psyche had already mapped out the territory of the human heart.

A person entering the desert on this inner journey searched for someone who could be a guide; someone who had learned the lessons of the desert; an elder whose experience might be of use to the young novice. The novice had one question to ask of the elder: How could he be saved?

In reply, these elders didn't say much and they wrote hardly anything. Their response was very short, usually laconic, sometimes difficult to understand and almost always directed personally to the monk. They certainly had no intention of being remembered or quoted. They just wanted to pass on to others what they had learned from their own hard-won experience. We may never have heard of these wise people of the Desert had it not been for the fact that some of their sayings, aimed at particular individuals in particular circumstances, at some stage were written down by disciples who didn't want their words of wisdom to be lost. These sayings now form a huge body of literature known as *The Sayings of the Desert Fathers*.

Macarius of Egypt was one of the best-known of these Desert Fathers. His life spanned the whole of the fourth century, which was the time when the Desert movement sprang up and flourished. Macarius was a contemporary of some of the great figures of the early Christian Desert era: Arsenius, John the Dwarf, Moses, Evagrius of Pontus. Many early figures knew, met or were influenced by Macarius: St Jerome, St Ephrem the Syrian, St John Cassian, Isaac of Nineveh, Palladius, Rufinus, Isaiah of Scetis and Barsanuphius.

The original Macarius – Macarius of Egypt – was a very attractive personality, and it's no surprise that someone may have wanted to write 'in his style' and even to assume his name. Such was this Syrian monk of the early fifth century, who is known today as the Pseudo-Macarius. Pseudo Macarius is best known for his Great Letter and for a collection of *Fifty Homilies*.

THE DIVIDED HEART

*The heart governs and reigns over the whole bodily organism;
and when grace possesses the ranges of the heart, it rules over
all the members and the thoughts. For there, in the heart, is the
mind, and all the thoughts of the soul and its expectation; and in
this way grace penetrates also to all the members of the body...
within the heart are unfathomable depths. There are reception
rooms and bedchambers in it, doors and porches, and many
offices and passages. In it is the workshop of righteousness and of
wickedness. In it is death; in it is life... the heart is Christ's palace:
there Christ the King comes to take His rest, with the angels and
the spirits of the saints, and He dwells there, walking within it
and placing His Kingdom there.*

*The heart is but a small vessel: and yet dragons and lions are
there, and there are poisonous creatures and all the treasures of
wickedness; rough, uneven paths are there, and gaping chasms.
There likewise is God, there are the angels, there life and the
Kingdom, there light and the apostles, the heavenly cities and the
treasures of grace: all things are there.*

Pseudo-Macarius, The Homilies: Hom. XV: 20, 32, 33

"GOD IS ALSO THERE"

Pseudo-Macarius was influenced by two spiritual giants: Origen and Gregory of Nyssa. From both of them he absorbed the Christian teaching that human beings are created in the image and likeness of God. In several places in his homilies, Pseudo-Macarius reminds us that our great dignity is that we are made in the image of God, and that this can never be lost. He is also careful to remind us of that other reality: our likeness to God is a more fragile reality and can be lost without due attentiveness.

Like all those great early Christian writers, Pseudo-Macarius was no hear-say writer. He knew what he was talking about. He writes out of an intuitive knowledge of human reality, carved out of his human experience. In using this image of the divided heart, the author is in harmony with the Desert Fathers and other early writers who see the human heart as a macrocosm, in which all reality is contained. These masters of the inner life deliberately turned the Greek philosophy of the person upside down. Greek philosophy saw the universe as a macrocosm, and the human person as a microcosm of that universe. The Desert tradition looks at it differently. The human person is the macrocosm, with everything that's real contained in the human heart. The world is only made up of rocks, seas, mountains, of thunderous elements and calm winds. That's nothing compared with what's inside the human heart.

But what exactly do the Scriptures and the early Christian writers mean when they talk of 'the heart'?

Modern language distinguishes three different activities of what we loosely call our 'soul' or our inner being: thinking, desiring and feeling. In this terminology we talk about three different faculties of the soul: the intellect, the will and the heart.

The Scriptures and the Desert tradition from which Pseudo-Macarius comes don't make these distinctions. They tend to speak of the human person that is visible to the eyes – the 'outer person'- and the part of the human person that's hidden to the eye – the 'inner person'.

We all know there's a difference between these two, and that they can even be in disharmony with each other. A person can speak and behave outwardly in a charitable manner, for example, but in his or her heart may harbour hatred.

So when the Scriptures and the Desert tradition speak of the human heart, they mean of course the physical organ of the heart, but they mean a lot more than that. As well as being the central and controlling element in our physical reality which directs all other organs of the body, the heart is where the intellect is situated. Scripture often refers to people thinking, feeling, or holding something "in the heart". In the Scriptures there is no separation between the head and the heart. We think with our heart. The psalmist puts it well: "May the thoughts of my heart be pleasing to thee." [26] When Scripture speaks of the heart it means the whole person. So, when Jesus says we are to love God "with all our heart" he means also "with all our soul, our mind and our strength". [27] The heart also includes what we now refer to as the unconscious. Further, the heart is our moral centre, the point where sin and grace meet. And finally, the heart is the point of self-transcendence, where we meet Christ. These five aspects – the heart as a physical organ, as the place where we think at our deepest level, as the centre of our unconscious, as the place where sin and grace meet, and finally as the place where we meet Christ – need to be held in continuous balance. The heart holds together the complete person. Pseudo-Macarius paints this picture well in the first paragraph of his image, when he indicates that when the heart is right, the whole body functions well.

He continues his image by drawing attention to something that each of us is painfully aware of from personal experience. There's something not right in us. Very soon in life we learn that however much we desire goodness, we are capable of doing wilful damage and harm to ourselves and to others. Another Desert Father, Diadochus of Photikē, puts it nicely. He says that our power of thinking has been split into two modes, and produces "at one and the same moment both good and evil thoughts, even against its own will". [28] The Russian writer Aleksandr Solzhenitzyn put it in a graphic way when he wrote in *The Gulag Archipelago* that "the line between good and evil passes through the human heart".

I clearly recall my first experience of sin. It's as clear to me now as it was on that day. I was scarcely 8 years old, and would have had no idea of the meaning of what we call sins: homicide, blasphemy, adultery, fornication, calumny or detraction. I couldn't have spelled the words, let alone understood what they meant. But on that day as I stood there in front of the person I had deliberately and calculatedly harmed in a mischievous way with my words, I knew what sin was and I knew that sin was in my heart.

When we realise that there's something wrong within us, and that there's probably no crime we couldn't personally commit, given the circumstances, we are beginning to understand at least half of the mystery of the human heart. The problem is that some of us stop there and spin out into self-concern and depression.

Pseudo-Macarius takes us out of this spin. He begins in his image with the negative, leaving the reader perhaps at the beginning with a sense of hopelessness. "There are dragons there and lions, and there are poisonous creatures; rough uneven paths and gaping chasms." We are appalled by what we see in our heart.

But then comes the hope. "There likewise is God, there are the angels, there life and the Kingdom, light, the apostles, the saints, the treasures of grace. All things are there."

This is typically Syrian in style. Just when we think we are overcome by what we see in ourselves, he raises us up and encourages us not to lose confidence. Isaac of Nineveh, another Syrian writer of the seventh century puts it this way:

> "Enter eagerly into the treasure-house that lies within you, and so you will see the treasure-house of heaven: for the two are the same, and there is but one single entry to them both. The ladder that leads to the Kingdom is hidden within you, and is found in your own soul. Dive into yourself and in your soul you will discover the rungs by which to ascend." [29]

This is one of the great aspects of truly Christian belief. It allows us to be real. It doesn't force us to imagine the journey as an impossible struggle to get rid of what is dark in us. It doesn't require a born-again hope and desire. It allows us to say "Kyrie Eleison – Lord have mercy" and then even in that moment to say, "And to God be the glory." In the truly Christian tradition, repentance and praise of God go hand in hand.

This truth is deeply embedded in the Desert tradition. People are sometimes disconcerted in reading the stories of the Desert Fathers and Mothers when they discover how often those giants of the Desert repeat their cries of repentance or affirmations of need. The reality is that these desert dwellers knew that in the very deepest part of their darkness they could confidently find Jesus the Lord of light waiting to bring healing. "Kyrie Eleison!" is not a cry of self-reproach, but a joyful recognition of Jesus as Lord, and a proclamation of the power of the Lord over sin and the darkness of the human heart.

In another part of his writings, Pseudo-Macarius uses another image. He compares our soul to a great city. At the centre of the city there is a beautiful castle. Near the castle is the market-place, and beyond that lie the suburbs. In his image the suburbs or the outskirts of the city represent the external senses. Often our troubles start right here, in what we allow ourselves to see or to touch or taste or smell or hear. And it is there that we are most often disturbed. But sometimes these disturbances reach the market place. The market is an image of the ante-chamber to the soul. Like any market-place this is the place where bargaining and trickery take place. What we have allowed in through our external senses now clamour for attention. They want to find their way into the inner court of the castle. It's here that one must be on guard and prevent these disturbing elements from slipping through the entrance into the inner courtyard.

This is why the Desert Fathers and Mothers were quick to teach their disciples one very significant lesson: one must be attentive. Anyone venturing into the desert knows that no one can survive there without constant attentiveness both to what is outside oneself and in particular to what is going on inside. One must keep an eye open for changes in the wind, the position of landmarks, tracks in the sand. But one must also be attentive to one's inner condition, to check one's stomach, one's mind, one's tendency to fantasise. The Desert Fathers and Mothers spoke of this attitude of attention as *agrypnia,* the spiritual attitude of wakefulness. Sometimes they use another word, *prosoch,* to describe this attitude of keeping watch over one's inward thoughts and the workings of the imagination.

More importantly, they spoke of the state opposite to this attitude of attentiveness, which they described as *prelest,* or spiritual drowsiness. *Prelest* was a sort of torpor, like the state of a person who is just waking up and is in no state to get moving. Resisting the pain of moving from the state of pleasant semi-consciousness to face the reality of the day ahead, we often say, "Just leave me alone for a little while; let me go back to sleep". This state of drowsiness is how many careless Christians live through each day, not noticing what is happening, and not recognising the signs of God in every moment. The Desert Fathers saw this state of sleep-walking through life as one of the deadliest enemies of the heart.

Against this they urged the attitude of attention, especially to what is going on inside. There are many stories which end with an elder saying to his young novice, "Watch yourself!" What the elder meant was that the novice must be careful not to lose contact with the currents moving within him. St Mark the Ascetic, in a letter to his disciple Nicolas, wrote: "Descend into the depths of the heart, and search out these three powerful giants of the demon: forgetfulness, laziness and ignorance..." [30] "Be attentive to yourself, guard your heart, don't grow listless" is a constantly repeated refrain. Evagrius of Pontus wrote: "Nothing is more essential to prayer than attentiveness." [31]

The writings of Pseudo-Macarius have had a profound effect on Christian spirituality, in both Eastern and Western Christianity. Even if many people have not heard of him, they have imbibed his spirituality through other significant preachers, writers and musicians. Reading him was a great liberation of spirit for Charles Wesley, the great Evangelical preacher and hymn-writer. He wrote in his diary for July 30th 1736, "I read Macarius and I sang." He was not the only one to discover the joy and enthusiastic love of Pseudo-Macarius' spirituality of the heart.

Pseudo-Macarius got it right in his image of the human heart. We don't need too much reminding of the bad news around us or within us. We desperately need to know the good news. Whatever else we may see in our heart – the beasts and wild things – we need to hold firmly to one conviction – God is there, and the angels, too.

Evagrius of Pontus

eople who lived in the times of the Desert Fathers and Mothers described the desert region, especially the desert of Egypt as "a vast and terrible wilderness". Anyone going into the desert could not expect to find comforts and distractions. Just silence and solitude. There were two possible outcomes for those who took up this life: one either went mad (and some did), or one became incredibly insightful and wise. There's plenty of evidence that many desert-dwellers came into this second category, as stories from the *Sayings of the Desert Fathers* indicate.

One of the most significant personalities of this Desert period was Evagrius of Pontus. He stands out because while most of the first generation of monks who went into the desert were simple and probably illiterate, Evagrius was a highly-educated, classical scholar. In his own lifetime he was known as a keen thinker, a polished speaker and a gifted writer. He was the first to record and systematise the oral teachings of the early monks. Fifteen hundred years before Sigmund Freud or Carl-Gustav Jung, Evagrius had written with great insight on dreams and their significance. Our present-day understanding of the 'seven deadly sins' owes its origins to what Evagrius called the *logismoi* or 'thoughts' which beset people engaged in the spiritual journey. His insight was the result of a hard-won battle with his own demons. When he wrote of the tricks of the mind and the ever-present risk of self-deception, he was writing from personal experience. He himself had gone down the track and he knew what he was talking about.

Most of what we know of Evagrius comes from the historian Palladius, who in 419 wrote a history of the monks of Egypt and Palestine, titled the *Lausiac History*. Having lived for nine years with Evagrius in Kellia, Palladius knew him well enough to be able to write about him with some authority. Palladius tells us that Evagrius was born in 345 in Ibora, a small town on the shores of the Black Sea, and that he died in the desert of Egypt in 399. His early life was influenced by many people whom the Church recognises as saints: he was instructed by St Gregory Nazianzen and he was ordained reader by St Basil the Great and deacon by St Gregory of Nyssa (380), whom he accompanied to the Second Council of Constantinople in 381.

Evagrius remained for a time as archdeacon in Constantinople. But during this time he fell in love with an upper-class woman, the wife of an important official. Evagrius decided to break off the affair, but as Palladius puts it the woman by now was "eager and frantic". One night Evagrius had a dream in which he saw himself arrested and in chains. In the dream an angel appeared to him and compelled him to swear on the Gospels that he would leave town. When he woke he decided to fulfil the oath he had sworn in the dream, and took the first available ship to Jerusalem where he found refuge in a monastery established by two significant personalities of this period, Rufinus and Melania.

He stayed there for a short time, but soon, Palladius tells us, vainglory and pride got the better of him. He fell ill, and it was only when he admitted that he had come to Jerusalem because of the fear of a personal scandal that he regained his health. Palladius writes:

> "Now when the doctors were in a quandary and could find no
> treatment to cure him, the blessed Melania addressed him: 'Son, I am
> not pleased with your long sickness. Tell me what is in your mind, for
> your sickness is not beyond God's aid.' Then he confessed the whole
> story. She told him: 'Promise by the Lord that you mean to aim at the
> monastic life, and even though I am a sinner, I will pray that you be

given a lease on life.' He agreed, and was well again in a matter of
days. He got up, received a change of clothing at her hands, then left
and took himself to the mountain of Nitria in Egypt." [32]

This was in 383. Evagrius lived at Nitria for two years, and then moved to Kellia, which is about 100km north of present-day Cairo. He lived here under the guidance of Macarius the Great for the last 14 years of his life.

Palladius tells us that to the end of his days Evagrius struggled with his demons, especially the temptation to pride and vainglory. There's a lovely story about this in the *Sayings of the Desert Fathers*:

> *"One day at the cells, there was an assembly about some matter or*
> *other and Abba Evagrius held forth. Then the priest said to him,*
> *'Abba, we know that if you were living in your own country you*
> *would probably be a bishop and a great leader; but at present you*
> *sit here as a stranger.' He was filled with compunction, but was not*
> *at all upset and bending his head he replied, 'I have spoken once and*
> *will not answer, twice but I will proceed no further' (Job 40.5)."* [33]

Evagrius passed on his firsthand knowledge of the spiritual journey to many disciples, and he became particularly well-known for his teaching on prayer. Some of his teaching became suspect because it was considered to reflect the teachings of Origen whose teachings had been condemned by the Sixth, Seventh, and Eighth Ecumenical Councils. Nevertheless Evagrius' teachings on asceticism, prayer, and the spiritual life had a profound impact upon both Christian East and West. One of his key disciples, John Cassian, established monasteries in southern France and adapted key Evagrian works for his Western audiences. Through Cassian these teachings passed to Benedict and have influenced the West. Evagrius has always been regarded as a master in the Eastern Church, and has profoundly influenced people such as John Climacus, Dionysius the Areopagite, Maximus the Confessor, Isaac of Nineveh, and Symeon the New Theologian.

THE PILGRIM

*You know very well, brother, that someone who wants to set
out on a long journey will first of all examine himself, and then
he will attach himself to other travellers with whom he is able
and willing to keep up; otherwise he may get left behind by his
companions on the journey and come to harm. Likewise, if people
who travel tire themselves out on the very first day by rushing
along, they will end up wasting many days as a result of sickness.
But if they start out walking at a gentle pace until they have got
accustomed to walking, in the end they will not get tired even
though they walk great distances.*

*It is exactly the same with a person who wants to travel on the
road to righteousness. First of all let him look into himself and
see how strong he is, then let him choose a way of life that is
appropriate to himself. It is better to begin from one's feeble state
and end up strong, to progress from small things to big, than to
set your heart from the very first on the perfect way of life, only
to have to abandon it later – or to keep to it solely out of habit,
because of what others will think – in which case all this labour
will be in vain.*

*Likewise, anyone who wishes to embark on the labours of the
virtuous life should train himself gently, until he finally reaches
the perfect state. Do not be perplexed by the many paths trodden
by our Fathers of old, each different from the other; do not
zealously try to imitate them all: this would only upset your way
of life. Rather, choose a way of life that suits your feeble state;
travel on that, and you will live, for your Lord is merciful and he
will receive you, not because of your achievements, but because of
your attention, just as he received the destitute woman's gift.*

Evagrius of Pontus, Admonition on Prayer

"Sing up – and keep on walking!"

The image of a journey is one of the more common themes in literature. Fairy stories, nursery rhymes, biographies and epic poems all count in their collection some works which have the theme of a journey which a hero figure undertakes, through difficult and dangerous experiences, until he reaches a time or a place of rest or conquest. We think of Virgil's *Aeneid*, Homer's *Odyssey*, Goethe's *Faust*, the *Grail* legends, the *Orpheus* myth or Tolkein's *Lord of the Rings*. One of the classic epic poems with this theme is Dante's famous work, *The Divine Comedy*, which is the imaginative story of Dante's journey through Hell and Purgatory to Paradise. John Bunyan's *Pilgrim's Progress* tells the story of Faithful's journey to Sion, the celestial city. Bunyan's opening lines are full of symbolism and meaning:

> "As I walked through the wilderness of this world, I lighted on a
> certain place ... and laid me down in that place to sleep;
> and as I slept I dreamed a dream..."

There's a common pattern in all these legends. They tell of heroes and heroines embarking on a journey that takes them from home, across dangerous thresholds, into new unexplored territories, and then back home with an expanded consciousness.

The three phases of this journey – departure, struggle, and return – are a metaphor for what happens to everybody who embarks on the less heroic but just as difficult journey through life, and especially to those who take up the longest journey of all, the journey inwards. This journey usually involves recurring patterns. At first we find ourselves in a state that's secure, and we feel grounded in the conviction that 'this is where I belong' in life. A moment comes when we experience painful disorientation. This can happen because of some crisis outside of ourselves – the death of someone close, departure of people we love, a breakdown in relationships, loss of home or job. Or it may be something internal, biological and unavoidable – like being born, or passing through adolescence, or reaching the time of menopause or the famous mid-life crisis. Finally, for most, there's the moment of being surprisingly re-oriented, and finding a new 'proper place'. Then the pattern soon recurs.

In the journey of life we have two tasks. One is a psychological work and the other is a spiritual work. Our psychological work concerns our conscious life. When our conscious life functions well it enables us to relate appropriately to others, to make assessments and judgments, to share feelings. When it functions badly it drives us to neurotic behaviours such as addictions, judgmental attitudes or irrational attachments. To a large extent our psychological work happens of itself by the process of living with others and surviving in a complex world. But there are other ways of assisting the process: reflecting on our experiences, meditation, bodily disciplines, imaging, poetry, music, art, etc. In our psychological work we are changed.

Our spiritual journey is different, but parallel. While in our psychological work we are changed, in our spiritual work we are *revealed* for what we are to ourselves and to others. Our spiritual work concerns our Self, which is the centre of our entire psyche. The Self creates a balance between all the opposing forces of the Ego. It is the Self which reconciles the tension between control and surrender, between revenge and forgiveness, between effort and letting go. Unfortunately, the forces and tensions created by what we call our psychological work take up so much of our energy that we have little time for the deeper, more significant and more enriching spiritual work. And yet it is here that we find the healing, wholeness and integration that bring about inner freedom. It's hard work, because it always means leaving something behind. Many of us fear taking even the first step.

In the hero fables, the call to begin the journey takes the form of a moment of loss, or the experience of failure or depression, an inner restlessness or an unexplained longing, a call to something beyond us or deeper inside us. When any of these experiences happen to us we know that we are being invited to make the journey. We are pilgrims on the threshold of the journey.

There are no broad and well-marked highways on this journey. Just signposts and notes, signs and symbols, images and hints left behind by others who have made their journey. These may help us.

They will give some focus to our sense of direction. But in the end each person's journey is unique.

It is not surprising that when many of the friends of God described their experience of the spiritual work they embarked on, they used the image of the pilgrim setting out on a journey. The image contains those elements of the 'search for the hidden treasure', the quest for a Holy Grail, the need to leave our places of comfort and security, the journey to an unknown land, the dangers of undertaking the quest, the need we have for some companionship on the way, the hardships we may encounter, the enemies who may block our path, the length of the journey, the dark nights we may encounter and the glimpses we get of our goal in the far distance.

When the Desert Fathers and Mothers fled into the deserts of Egypt and Syria in the fourth and fifth centuries, they may have had all manner of different reasons for doing so: disillusionment, flight from a decadent society, dissatisfaction with personal conditions or a personal crisis. But deep down they chose to go into these places because the physical wilderness of Egypt or Sinai or Syria mirrored the inner wilderness of their hearts, and the beasts that they might encounter in the desert resembled the inner demons they were to face.

Soon two schools of thought grew among these desert-dwellers. One stressed the need for stability, to "stay in one's cell", avoiding the temptation to keep moving in search of peace which can only be found within. Abba Ammonas and others considered it preferable to "stay seated in one's cell, to eat a little each day, and to have always in one's heart the words of the Publican – 'Lord be merciful to me, a sinner'". Ammonas warns against a practice which could (and in the Desert tradition certainly did) develop, of aimless wandering without any inner compass-point. These men and women became known as the *gyrovages*.

Abba Nilos on the other hand, puts before us the radical nature of the life of a pilgrim, one who is condemned, or who condemns himself, to live in a land that is not his own, among a people who are not his people and who have a language that is not his own, depending on hospitality given by others. These wanderers remind us that living a spiritual life means being permanently unsettled, never fully at home where one finds oneself.

In the end, 'staying in one's cell' or being a nomad amount to the same thing. Whatever way we look at it, the journey is always in two directions. It's a journey outwards, to something beyond us, but it's also a journey inwards, because it involves reflection, transformation within ourselves. In getting near our outward goal, we also discover that we are getting close to an inward goal and we discover that "hidden self" in us which St Paul talks about. When the friends of God use images of a journey to describe their experience, they use both 'outer images' such as the mountain or the exodus to the Promised Land, and 'inner images' such as the ladder going inwards or the spiral going downwards. When St Teresa uses the image of the interior castle she combines these two features of the journey inwards and outwards.

Ulysses left the familiar comforts of Ithaca thinking his journey was to Troy, only to find that his real journey was to come back as a wise, experienced and compassionate king. The prodigal son left the familiar routine of his father's house, thinking that his journey would take him to "a far-off country", when in fact the path led him back to where he started, but now able to give and receive love in a way that his older brother never succeeded in doing.

In some of his poems, T.S. Eliot uses words and images to evoke this sense of a journey which we undertake, departing, wandering, returning to where we started and knowing the place for the first time; facing the danger of having the experience but missing its meaning. His poem, *The Journey of the Magi*, captures this experience profoundly. In the poem, Eliot puts himself in the place of one of the Wise Men who reflects on the experience of his journey to Bethlehem. He says it was:

> *"Just the worst time of the year for a journey, and such a long*
> *journey. The ways deep and the weather sharp*
> *The very dead of winter...."*

There was every reason for not starting the journey at all. He ponders how at times the three travellers looked back over their shoulder at the secure life they had left behind, "the summer palaces on slopes, the terraces and the silken girls bringing sherbet". He tells how they arrived and discovered the Child in the stable, and how the experience changed him. He was different now. He could no longer live his former life:

> *"No longer at ease here, in the old dispensation, With an alien people,*
> *clutching their gods."*

A careful reading of Evagrius' image uncovers the wisdom he offers us. A wise pilgrim takes stock of his or her personal resources and makes sure that the goal and exigencies of the journey are not beyond those resources. A wise pilgrim stays with others; these companions may be able to give some good practical advice. And even though each one's journey will be different, it is not wise to separate oneself from the company of others. I like especially Evagrius' advice to be realistic and gentle with oneself. In the Desert tradition the older and wiser monks were always suspicious of the eager novice who wanted to race ahead and overextend himself. They had some good techniques for bringing such a person down to earth. Evagrius gives us a good hint: the important thing in this journey of ours is not to reach a destination as quickly as possible, but to learn the lessons that the experience of making the journey gives us.

Taking up the journey is what the Desert Fathers called *metanoia*, or conversion. Conversion is a firm resolution to point one's nose in a definite direction, and to make sure one's feet are pointing in the same direction. The effort, the struggle against self-deception or reluctance that this takes is a fierce challenge, but it leads to integration. An alternative to *metanoia* is *paranoia*, which in the end is madness.

One thing that Evagrius and others recommend to anyone taking up the journey is to travel light, meaning that we travel with few things that weigh us down, and that we walk lightly, with a song in our hearts. We remember the great spiritual pilgrim Mary, whose journey to her cousin Elizabeth was set in the framework of her prayer of thanks – the "Magnificat". Thanksgiving keeps us looking at the gifts of God and keeps us positive and hopeful. St Augustine has a beautiful way of expressing this:

> "O children of peace, walk in the way that is Christ!
> Sing on the way as pilgrims do to console themselves in the fatigue of the journey.
> Sing on the way!
> I implore you, through him who is our way, sing a new song!
> Do not sing those old songs, harping on the same tune.
> Instead, sing the love song of your homeland!
> Do not sing even one old tune!
> Since you are a new person, walking on a
> new path, Sing up – and keep on walking!"[34]

John Cassian

t's one of the quirks of history that sometimes people whose ideas or actions have made an impact on the lives of others remain almost unknown even to those whose lives they have influenced. John Cassian was one of these people. Cassian's writings were considered essential reading in the early Church, and those same writings continue to influence people, consciously or not, right up to today. Yet not many people – at least in the Western Church – would remember him, recognise his name, or know anything of his writings.

The details of Cassian's life are sketchy. What we know of his life comes from fragments of his writings and the writings of others which help build up at least a broad framework of his life story.

He was apparently born around the year 360 in Scythia Minor, now Dobrudja, on the border of modern-day Romania and Bulgaria. Most likely he was born into a Christian family, and he had at least one sister. His family had great holdings of land and few material worries. Because of this, he was well-educated and able to travel.

When he was a young man, he and an older friend, Germanus, travelled to Bethlehem where they entered a monastery near to the cave of the birth of Jesus. They spent three years in the monastery, and during that time they began to hear stories of the lives and words of the monks in Egypt. This inspired them to go and see for themselves what was happening in the desert. The two friends took an oath that they would not needlessly lengthen their stay, but would return as soon as possible. However, they were so attracted by the lives of these solitaries that they obtained permission to remain longer in the desert. They remained there for about 15 years, and it was during this time that Cassian collected material on the lives and teachings of the holy monks.

Around 399 Cassian and Germanus fled the desert during a time of stormy religious controversy and travelled to Constantinople where they lived with the great John Chrysostom. Cassian was ordained a deacon at that time. When John Chrysostom was forced into exile from Constantinople in 404, Cassian, being a speaker of Latin, was sent to Rome to plead the cause of Chrysostom before the Pope, Innocent I. Cassian was probably ordained a priest while he was in Rome.

He didn't stay long in Rome, but moved to Marseilles in southern France, and there he established two monasteries, one for men and one for women. From this time until his death, hardly anything is known of him. He died in Marseilles in 435.

It was only about twenty-five years after his experience in the desert that Cassian wrote down his recollections of the lives and sayings of the monks of Egypt, and he wrote them specifically for the monks of France. While we can safely assume that his recollections reflect faithfully the spirituality of the Desert Fathers and Mothers, it is clear that they also reflect his personal spirituality.

Between 420 and 429 Cassian wrote two major spiritual works, called the *Institutions* and the *Conferences*. According to his explanation, the *Institutions* deal with external matters such as the organisation of the community, while the *Conferences* deal with the personal life of the monk: his training in community life and prayer.

The *Conferences* are presented in the form of twenty-four conversations that he and his friend Germanus had with the greatest of the Egyptian *abbas*. They also summarise what Cassian remembers as the principles of the spiritual and ascetic life.

The first four books of the *Institutions* deal with the rules governing monastic life; the remaining eight books deal with the eight principal challenges the monk faces in his spiritual journey: gluttony, impurity, covetousness, anger, dejection, listlessness, vainglory and pride.

Cassian wrote a third work, *On the Incarnation of the Lord,* which was a defence of orthodox doctrine against the views of Nestorius.

Cassian's *Conferences* and *Institutions* are considered to be the greatest body of teaching on spirituality to come out of the age of the Desert Fathers. In particular, St Benedict made use of Cassian in writing his Rule, and laid down that selections from the *Conferences* should be read each day in all his monasteries. This is how Cassian's writings have had such an influence on Western spirituality.

It is strange, then, that he is hardly known or recognised in the West except in the limited circle of monastic spirituality. This could be explained at least partly by the fact that Cassian was regarded as dangerously close to two currents of heretical thinking.

In the first place, he was thought to be sympathetic to the doctrine of Origen whose teaching caused conflict and dissension among the monks of Egypt, provoking a great exodus of monks from the desert. Aspects of Origen's teaching were condemned in 543.

In the second place, Cassian is considered to be associated with what became known as semi-Pelagianism. This view tried to establish a middle way between the views of St Augustine and of Pelagius on the topic of grace and free will. While Augustine emphasised the role of original sin in human life, and the absolute need for grace in order to be saved, Pelagius had emphasised the human person's capacity to attain salvation through personal effort. Cassian tried to take a middle road. He did not deny the Fall through original sin. But he maintained that even after the Fall there still remained in every soul "some seeds of goodness... implanted by the kindness of the Creator" which, however, must be "brought to life by the assistance of God".

This view – semi-Pelagianism – was condemned by the Latin Church in the Council of Orange in 529, a century after Cassian's death. Since this council was not an Ecumenical Council, the Eastern Church has never regarded Cassian as heretical, and in fact recognises him as "St Cassian the Roman".

THE PLOUGHMAN

The farmer, for instance, does not shirk the burning rays of the sun or the frosts and the ice as he tirelessly cuts through the earth, as, over and over again, he ploughs the untamed sods of the field. All the time he pursues his objective, cleaning all the brambles from the field, clearing away all grass, breaking up the earth until it is like fine sand. He is aware that there is no other way to achieve his aim, which is the prospect of an abundant harvest and a rich yield of crops so that he may live securely or add to his possessions. He draws the grain willingly from the fullness of his barns and, working intensively, he invests it in the loosened soil. He pays no attention to what he is losing now because he is thinking ahead to the coming harvests.

John Cassian, Conferences 1 Chapter II

"Keep the goal in view"

Bookstores, especially in the English-speaking world, are stacked with books about leadership and visionary administration, about personal motivation and group animation, about decision-making and goal-setting. Authors present memorable catch-phrases such as "the most important thing is to know what is the most important thing", or "the main task is to keep the main task the main task", or "first things first", or "keep the goal in view". They remind us to "begin as you want to continue, because the way you will continue is the way you have begun". Titles of books indicate their theme: "Finding True North", "Mindfulness", "Dreams and Living". In many bookstores the section on leadership and management is near or next to the section on "self-help", "personal fulfillment", "spirituality" or "religion".

Monks of the fourth century might not be so surprised to discover this. For them, the two things – living spiritually and living effectively – went together. Modern authors and readers might be surprised, though, to discover that many of the insights and the pithy catch-phrases in these modern books had already been coined back in the fourth century.

Evagrius of Pontus was the first to write about the significance of dreams as an index of one's deepest personal life. Evagrius wrote a good deal about the importance of self-awareness, which he called "mindfulness". One of the great pieces of advice given by the early Desert Fathers and Mothers to their disciples was "watch yourself!" And John Cassian's first chapters in his book of *Conferences* concerned the need to keep the goal of life in view. His image of the farmer was supplemented by other images: the good businessman, the man-of-war, the bowman. The lesson behind the images was the same: know what you are aiming for.

Having lived with the monks of Egypt for many years, and having been impressed by their way of life, Cassian wanted his monks in France to hear the voices of the great monks of the Egyptian desert. In his *Institutions* and *Conferences*, Cassian employs a literary technique:

he writes his *Conferences* as if they were talks given by some of the great existing or historical personalities of the desert – Abba Moses, Abba Serapion, Abba Antony, Abba Isaiah. Did these particular Abbas really say what is attributed to them? It really doesn't matter. What matters is that Cassian is faithful to the Desert tradition which he found so impressive.

Cassian is writing for monks. He's clear that monastic life is an "art or a discipline with its own methods".[37] Much of his writing consists of instructions to monks in monasteries on how they should behave. These details probably don't touch the lives of people like us who do not live in monasteries. However, Cassian is a pragmatist who combines both the ideal and the real, and for that reason the principles he lays down are just as relevant then as they are to us today.

In the first of his *Conferences*, he spells out the fundamental issue: know what you are aiming for, and keep the goal in view. Significantly, the Abba to whom he attributes this Conference was Abba Moses, who was one of the truly great personalities of the Desert, known for his passion and for his compassion. In his former life he was a robber and a murderer. He knew what passion was about, and he knew what dramatic and dangerous lengths he could go to in order to achieve his goals. After his conversion he became known for his refusal to judge his fellow monks. Though he was a murderer in his past life, he desired to be a martyr for the Lord. He died in the year 405 at the age of 75-- murdered when his monastery was attacked by bandits.

Moses becomes the spokesperson for Cassian's first lesson in the spiritual life. In his talk with Cassian and his companion Germanus, Moses uses two Greek words, *telos* and *skopos*, to describe this first task of setting one's goals. *Telos* is what Moses calls the "ultimate end", the long-term aim of anyone who takes up an enterprise. Using the image of a farmer or a ploughman, Moses describes the ultimate end of the farmer as living at ease with a good harvest. For the farmer this ultimate end, this *telos*, is a matter of life and death. Once this is lost, there's no central point, and – for the farmer – no motivation to endure the hard work of ploughing the soil, or working hard day after day in the scorching heat or bitter frost.

But a long-term end is by its nature a distant reality, and it can easily move off our screen. The wise farmer, keeping in mind his long-term end, puts before himself some short-term or immediate goals. This is what Moses describes as the *skopos*. In the image he uses, the *skopos* of the farmer is the hard work of ploughing the earth: breaking up the clods of earth, clearing it of briars and weeds, and making it fine and fertile so that it can yield a good harvest. This activity of ploughing the field is not the ultimate end. It is a necessary means to that end, but in itself it is secondary, and a wise farmer doesn't get the two things confused. The purpose of the farmer's life is not to plough fields, but to get a good harvest.

The farmer also needs to have useful instruments to help cultivate the soil (his *skopos*) in order to get a good harvest (his *telos*). He needs a good sharp plough, and he needs healthy animals to draw the plough. These instruments all need to be kept in good order. Without good tools and healthy animals he can't achieve his purposes. But important as this is, keeping his tools in good order is not the ultimate goal of the farmer. His tools serve a higher purpose.

Cassian then draws out the lesson for his monks, using Moses as his mouthpiece. The *telos* of the monk is the attainment of paradise. That is the ultimate aim of all his life. The *skopos* of the monk is what leads him to this ultimate aim, and he calls this goal "purity of heart". Purity of heart, for Cassian and for other Desert writers, was the state of single-minded and clear-sighted search for God. It was the state of simplicity. And the means to achieve this state of purity of heart is the set of practices that every monk would have understood: prayers, fasting, mortification, vigils and almsgiving.

These activities are ways in which the immediate goal of the monk – purity of heart – can be achieved. And this, in its turn, is the step towards the monk's ultimate aim – paradise. Cassian uses another telling illustration to describe this process. He writes of a marksman who wants to prove to his master that he is a skilled shooter. That is his *telos*. He does this by firing accurately at the target. That's his *skopos*. Without the target, his arrows fly everywhere and nowhere. But he also needs a good bow and sharp arrows to perform his skill.

Similarly, continues Moses in Cassian's *Conferences*, the things a monk uses – fasting, saying prayers, practising asceticism – serve the purpose of helping a monk to achieve purity of heart, which ultimately brings him to the state of paradise. But these methods or instruments are not ends in themselves. Moses recounts stories of monks who lost sight of their ultimate purpose, and made their feats of asceticism, hours of prayer, vigils or fasting their ultimate goal. They came to grief either through pride or discouragement. "Keep the aim in view", warns Moses.

This is just as useful to us in the twenty-first century as it was to the monks of the fourth century. It is easy to lose sight of the long-term goal of our Christian life, and so lose contact with the 'true north' of our lives. Our modern-day books on leadership tell us: "If you don't know where you want to go, the chances are that you will end up getting there – that is, nowhere'.' This is good advice for the Christian journey as well. It is easy to get distracted on the journey by the many good, no-ble, important, fascinating things that cross our path. It is even easier to limit our focus to the externals of Christian life, the performance of 'Christian actions', and lose sight of the goal or the end.

How does one keep on task? How does one not get too distracted? Once again, Cassian, the pragmatist, comes to our aid. Like his teacher Evagrius of Pontus, Cassian proposes that the main thing we have to deal with is our thoughts. It is thoughts, not feelings, that really trip us up. It's thoughts that remain in our heads and become obsessive. It's thoughts that evolve into behaviours.

Like Evagrius, Cassian teaches us that our thoughts come to us in three ways – either they are from God, from the devil or from our-selves. The key is to know how to recognise which thoughts come from where. Here again, Cassian comes to our aid. The second of his *Confer-ences* deals with *diakrisis,* or discrimination. *Diakrisis* is a spiritual gift which enables a person to discriminate between the kinds of thoughts that enter one's mind, to assess them accurately and to treat them ac-cordingly. It is the art of working out whether the thoughts that come into one's head are friendly or fatal. It is the art of knowing which side these thoughts are on. It is the art of knowing which thoughts should be allowed to take up residence in our minds and which ones should be quickly and effectively moved on from.

To illustrate his point, Cassian has Moses put before his two lis-teners the image of a money-changer. When a money-changer is pre-sented with a bag of money by some crafty trader, he has to be able to work out what is counterfeit and what is valid currency. An astute money-changer learns to recognise the genuineness of the coins by their shape, by the image that is on the coin, by the weight of the coin and by the lustre of the coin.

Cassian suggests that we apply these same four tests to our thoughts, confronting them with the following questions: Is this thought the right shape – that is, is it filled with what is genuinely good for everyone? Secondly, whose image is on it – that is, does this thought come from the Lord Jesus and lead me genuinely to work for Him or for someone else? Thirdly, does it have the weight of faith and the tradition of the Church behind it? And finally, has vanity or self-interest crept into this thought, diminishing its lustre? It is a rather quaint illustration, but it's a very practical and easy-to-manage way of testing one's thoughts to see whether they are to be followed or not.

At the end of this *Conference*, Cassian puts into the mouth of Moses two pieces of advice which I find both encouraging and challenging. In speaking of the dangers that are involved in the spiritual journey, and of the likelihood that a pilgrim will get lost or distracted on the way, Moses suggests that it is the truly humble person who is saved from this possibility. This is because a humble person is not afraid to risk self-disclosure, and a humble person is not afraid to ask the advice of the wise.

It doesn't take much skill to recognise in the two words that Cassian uses, *telos* and *skopos*, the words that make up our English word 'telescope'. The function of a telescope is to bring into close focus something that is distant to view, and to help a person find the right course to follow. That's exactly what Cassian means in proposing his image of the ploughman.

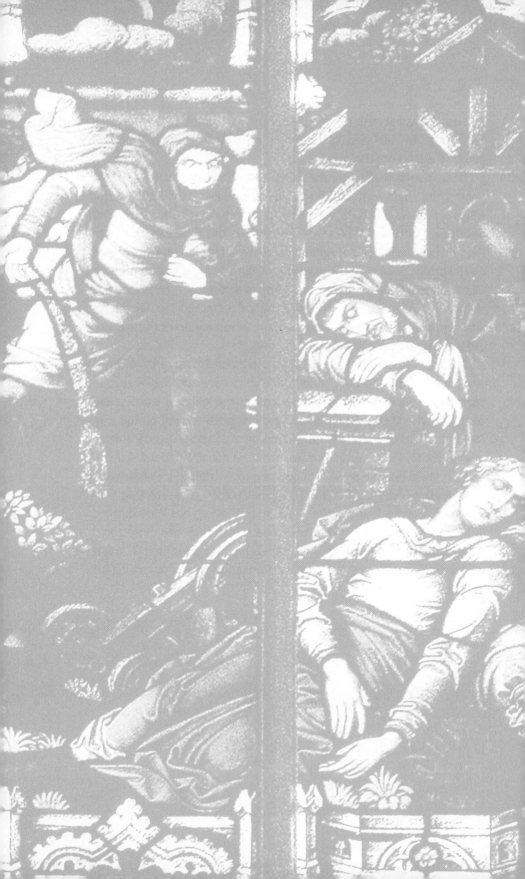

Dante Alighieri

hen a nation refers to one of its significant people simply by the title "The ..." you know that the person holds a prime place in that nation's life and history. Among all the poets of Italian literature, only one is referred to as "The" poet: Dante Alighieri.

Dante is beyond doubt the greatest of Italian poets. Many would say he was one of the greatest poets that Western civilization has produced. The Irish poet William Butler Yeats called him "the chief imagination of Christendom" and T. S. Eliot claimed that "Dante and Shakespeare divide the modern world between them. There is no third".

Dante was born in Florence in 1265. His family was of ancient nobility; though they were not wealthy land-owners, they were part of the economic life of the city. His mother Donna Gabriella degli Abati died when Dante was a child. His father, Alighiero di Bellincione Alighieri, was a lawyer and died when Dante was 18.

When Dante was barely nine years old, a significant event occurred which profoundly affected his life. He caught a glimpse of a girl whom he names as Beatrice, and fell instantly in love with her. From this first meeting with Beatrice, to the second, nine years later, when a greeting from the "wonderful lady" left the young poet "as if intoxicated", love for this woman completely dominated Dante and almost destroyed his talents. In his whole life Dante caught sight of Beatrice only three times, and never spoke to her. Her death in 1290 almost sent the poet out of his mind. The memory of Beatrice remained with him all his life and she became for him a personification of all that is pure, of all that is symbolised by heaven. Beatrice became a key figure in his most famous work, *The Divine Comedy*.

A 'comedy', as traditionally defined, is a story that "begins in sorrow and ends in joy", Dante called his work simply *The Comedy*. Later Italian writers called it *The Divine Comedy*, and that is how it is known today. It is not clear when Dante began this masterpiece. It appears that he finished the first of its three parts by 1314, and the last shortly before his death on 14 September 1321.

The plot of *The Divine Comedy* is straightforward. It begins with Dante lost in a Dark Wood, unable to remember how he got there or how long he has been walking. He sees a mountain and sets out to climb it, but he is driven back by three beasts that bar his path. He meets the poet Virgil who tells him he must make a journey through hell to purgatory and finally to heaven. Virgil promises to accompany him on the journey.

Descending into the dark wood where the sun is silent, they come to the gates of hell, above which are written the words: *Abandon hope, all ye who enter here.*

The residents in hell are historical persons known to Dante. No one is spared: poets and philosophers, emperors and politicians, merchants, public figures, men and women, the famous and the infamous – popes too are found in parts of hell. As we read the poem, we soon realise that 'hell' in the poem is an image of the possibilities of evil within ourselves. In a symbolic way, these people represent the disordered desires in our lives, and as we plunge deeper and deeper into our inner self, we recognise this clearly. Hell in Dante's poem is not a place of punishment to which anybody is sent arbitrarily. Hell is the condition to which we reduce ourselves by a stubborn decision to choose ourselves rather than others. Hell – or heaven for that matter – is living for eternity the way we lived during our life.

Like the Mikado in Gilbert and Sullivan's comic opera, Dante "makes the punishment fit the crime". The thief who robbed others of their possessions is now victim to others who can take away his appearance and make him invisible. Sowers of discord, who divide families, people, and the state, are constantly split in two by a demon with a sword. Hypocrites walk around in cloaks which are magnificently embroidered on the outside, but have lead inside, making any sort of progress impossible. Sorcerers who have attempted to take over God's role by trying to pry into the future are punished by having their face and feet point in opposite directions.

Emerging from hell, Dante leads his readers through purgatory towards heaven, where he meets Beatrice and is led by her to St Bernard, who obtains for Dante, through the intercession of Mary, the grace of understanding the mysteries of our faith. Beatrice becomes what she had been at the beginning for Dante, the symbol of pure love.

The poem is a comment on the political, scientific, and philosophical thought of the time, and may be interpreted on four levels: the literal, allegorical, moral, and mystical. Dante uses himself as a symbol of 'everyman' in a journey through life. The poem is also a vehicle for Dante to make social comment. His use of symbolism is so dense and complex that hardly anyone today would be able to understand all the subtle references he makes to people and events of his day.

Dante's account of his descent and his ascent is the story of his journey through self-knowledge to the experience of God. It is also the story of the spiritual journey each of us makes through darkness into light. "The way up is the way down." The spiritual journey each of us makes will lead us downwards, into the depths of our beings, so as to ascend, purified through love, to the enjoyment of God.

A striking image Dante uses at the very beginning of his Divine Comedy is the account of his meeting with three beasts who stand in his path, testing his courage as he sets out, and reminding him that we cannot set out on our journey inwards without meeting our personal demons.

THE BEASTS AT THE GATE

Midway this way of life we're bound upon,
I woke to find myself in a dark wood
Where the right road was wholly lost and gone.

And then, almost at the beginning of the rise
I faced a spotted leopard, all tremor and flow

And gaudy pelt. And it would not pass, but stood
so blocking my every turn that time and again
I was on the verge of turning back to the wood.

And then I shook with dread
at the sight of a great lion that broke upon me
raging with hunger, its enormous head

Held high as if to strike a mortal terror
into the very air. And down his track
a She-Wolf drove upon me, a starved horror
ravening and wasted beyond all belief.

She seemed a rack for avarice, gaunt and craving
Oh many the souls she has brought to endless grief!

Dante Alighieri, The Divine Comedy

"Here be monsters!"

One of the largest medieval maps of the world is found in the Victoria and Albert Museum in London. It measures two metres long and three metres high. Like all the earliest maps, it doesn't necessarily represent geographical or topographical reality. The world is flat; at the top of the map is a face, at the bottom are two feet and there are hands on the left and right-hand side. At the centre of the map is Jerusalem, and everything radiates from there. One soon realises that for the medieval Christian, the world was the body of Christ; the centre of the world was the land where Jesus lived, and everything else radiated from that. Today of course we have more accurate ways of seeing our world. But what's interesting is that in these early maps there was always a part set aside called *terra incognita* – unknown land – and frequently there was a little sign warning: "Here be monsters!"

Anyone who begins the journey into the uncharted regions of the inner self soon comes to the realisation: "Here be monsters." Dante's image of the three beasts standing at the gate describes the first and most important task of the pilgrim.

In Dante's poem, the three beasts standing guard at the gate are the leopard, the lion and the she-wolf. Through them, Dante introduces the reader to the three types of sin besetting people at the three significant stages of life: youth, adulthood and old age.

The leopard represents the hot-blooded sins of youth: impetuosity and weakness of will, self-indulgence and sexual gratification, wasteful spending and gluttony. Dante places these people in what he calls "upper hell", the least painful part of hell.

The lion symbolises the sins of adulthood: pride and violence. Dante places these people in the "first nether world". In this part of hell we find heretics: those who are violent against their neighbours or against themselves, and those who are violent towards art and nature.

The she-wolf guards the entrance to the "second nether world". In this part of hell we find those who have succumbed to the cold-blooded sins frequently found in the latter time of life: sins of greed or hoarding, sins of a twisted intellect such as fraud, sowing of discord, paranoid unforgiveness, lying, and twisting the truth about oneself or others. This is the place of deception.

Finally, there is the "third nether world" which needs no guard. We are at the bottom of the pit where the entry ticket is cold and cruel egotism, where even the passions of self-indulgence and anger are frozen into immobility – that is the final state of sinfulness.

How do we read Dante's image today? Does it belong in the same category as the medieval maps of the world – an interesting but now unenlightened view of humanity? Frankly, I have no trouble living with what Dante is trying to get at. In terms more familiar to us today, he is talking about what we call the 'shadow' part of ourselves: that side of us we would rather not face, own or admit to. Yet, as we mature, we realise that we must face this shadow part of ourselves or risk being destroyed by it. Many of us can remember watching stunned as Richard Nixon, President of the United States, was destroyed by the very thing he feared most and would not admit to – his fear of failure. Dante's image of the beasts is not so far from our experience at all.

In 1989 the city of Boston was shaken by what seemed to be a horrendous crime perpetrated on the night of 22 October. Charles Stuart, driving his pregnant wife from a pre-natal class, phoned the police frantically on his car telephone, reporting that his car had been stopped, his wife robbed of jewellery, and that he and his wife had been shot by the attacker. His wife, her head blasted open, was pulled from the bloodstained front seat of the couple's Toyota. Charles Stuart himself needed two operations, ten days in intensive care, and six weeks in hospital to recover from wounds that damaged his bowels, gall bladder and liver. Carol, his wife, died from the shooting. Her son, delivered through Caesarian section, also died after 17 days. People were horrified by the crime; their emotions caught by the senseless murder and destruction of what they thought were 'the perfect couple'.

Charles Stuart held his son Christopher for the last time from his hospital bed, and sent a message to be read at his wife's funeral: "You have brought joy and kindness to every life you've touched. Now you sleep away from me. I will never again know the feeling of your hand in mine."

The attacker was named by Stuart as a "raspy-voiced black man dressed in a jogging suit". The evidence set off a hunt for the killer, and brought to a head a great deal of beneath-the-surface racism.

The city was even more shocked some weeks later at the news that Stuart had jumped from a bridge to his death. Shock turned to outrage as they learned that Stuart, presumed innocent, was in fact the perpetrator of the crime, and that in order to claim a massive insurance he had taken out on his wife, he had murdered her and their child, shot himself to feign a struggle, and named a coloured man as the perpetrator of the crime.

Was this an act of a psychotic, or a man like us who had never dealt with the massive forces that drove him through his life, especially the forces of greed and pride? Stuart's background seemed an unlikely seed-bed for such a monstrous act. He grew up in a blue-collar suburb, went to a Catholic school. He began his working life as a cook where he met his future wife Carol. But already Stuart's greed and his need to advance beyond his origins were taking over. Finally, it overpowered him, and he planned the grisly crime that was to make him rich; he then destroyed his own life when he found the plan had back-fired.

While we may recoil from the horror of all that took place in that incident, most of us can recognise in it simply a horrendous magnification of the sorts of compromises, struggles with greed, pride, lust, or power that we are all exposed to. And in that incident we find the drama of one who throughout his life refused to look his 'beasts' in the eye, and was eventually overtaken by them.

The ancient Fathers of the Desert had a word to describe the attitude of the Christian to this experience: *Nepsis*. *Nepsis* means watchfulness. It describes the attitude of those who are on the watch against the beasts that beset them in the normal course of life: ego-preoccupation, consumerism, and compulsive living. Like Dante's beasts at the gate, these beasts are there waiting for us. No negotiating or bargaining or debate is going to free us from them. Nor will we ever be able to say that we have them under control. But to be afraid of them is as bad as, or worse than, treating them as tame pets. "Watch yourself", the constant cry of the old Desert Fathers, is as relevant today as it ever was.

The great gift of Christianity is that it allows us to face all this darkness and yet not be afraid. The Good News is that God, in Jesus and the Spirit, meets us at our point of greatest need. The Jews of the Old Testament found God in the desert, not at the end of their journeys. Jesus called Lazarus out of the tomb of death into new life, met the sinful woman in her moment of greatest shame and appeared to his disciples in the middle of the storm.

All this rings familiarly with modern understanding of human growth which reassures us that the shadow, when owned, becomes pure gold, but when disowned, it becomes the force which topples us. The deepest and darkest side of ourselves will often hold the seeds of a new life. Ernest Hemingway wrote: "Life breaks all of us, but some people grow at the broken places." Those who are most real are those who have not been afraid to face their brokenness or let others see it.

I lived in a community with a man who suffered what we might term a 'breakdown'. If he were alive today he would probably say that particular moment in his life was not a break-*down*, but a break-*through* in his life. But we watched as he seemed to unravel on the inside. One day I noticed that he had posted on his door a line from Psalm 107: "But who will bring me face-to-face with Edom?" It was a cry from the depths of his darkness. Paradoxically, it was during this time of deepest inner darkness that he was able to connect with others in a way he had never done before, or that we, his peers, could never do. This man's unexpected death brought about a surge of emotion from people of all ages and walks of life. Of all the things that were said about him at his funeral, the most powerful and most real tribute came from someone who said "He faced his demons".

As I've grown older and made an attempt at this journey inwards – many times turning back to 'safer' places – I have discovered aspects of myself I hadn't previously known.

I discover first of all that I'm one whole person in whom good and bad mingle together, and I realise that there are demons in my life that can't be cast out. I realise that God is found in the midst of the mixture of good and bad.

I discover that in this relationship of good and evil co-habiting within us, one's shadow is cast by a positive reality, and that dealing with that shadow should not eliminate the positive quality that casts the shadow.

I discover that much of my adult sinfulness is a consequence of childhood needs that haven't been met or faced. In some of my adult sins I can hear the voice from my childhood crying out for attention, or affection, or the approval of someone else.

I discover that the deeper function of my sinfulness is to teach me, and that before I try to do away with these dark or sinful parts of me I need to let them teach me. If not, the same patterns will continue to manifest themselves through my life.

In his play *After the Fall*, Arthur Miller describes the complex relationship between Quentin and Maggie, a relationship that reflects his own relationship with Marilyn Monroe, whom he had married. The stage set resembles Quentin's inner being, and the characters symbolise his memories and relationships. In one scene, Holga, who has preserved a spirit of hope despite having been through the atrocities of forced labour during the war, says to Quentin:

"For a long time after the War I kept having the same dream. It was a terrible time –
I came very close to not wanting to live.
I dreamed I'd given birth to an idiot child. And I kept running from it, it was horrible, that face... But one night it came again... and it suddenly... resembled me. It looked human. It moved me. And I kissed it. (Slight pause). It was my life."

There comes a time when we are invited to kiss what seems most repugnant in ourselves. Fables of every culture are full of stories of the transformation that takes place when someone who is ugly is kissed and accepted.

"The dragon sits by the side of the road, watching those who pass. Beware lest he devour you. We go to the Father of Souls, but it is necessary to pass by the dragons." – St Cyril of Jerusalem

The Psalmist

 book dealing with the images used to describe the journey to God would be incomplete without reference to the Book of Psalms, that unique collection of poetry, song and mystical reflection, which has been called the "song-book of the Church".

Actually, the Book of Psalms is not a book. Rather it is a collection of several books, spanning many centuries, from c. 1100 BCE to 400 BCE. It includes songs of lament, songs of praise, songs of thanksgiving, songs recalling history, songs of trust and liturgical songs.

The psalms are not doctrinal statements or creeds, and they are not a source of handy pick-me-ups and one-liners. The psalms are songs about people and their journey to and with God. These songs grew out of the lives of the people; they used them to reflect their praise of God and their inner experiences of joy, sorrow, anger, frustration, repentance, fear, praise, thanksgiving, trust and worship.

The best way to view the psalms is to see them as a document of the community of faith, in much the same way as, for example, Charles Wesley's classic hymn. *And can it be* expresses a whole view of life in response to God's action, and has become a confession of faith in song. Through the psalms we come face-to-face with our Maker and Redeemer. At the end, whatever emotion the psalm may have evoked or expressed, we are left thinking, "O Lord, our God, how great is your name through all the earth!" (Ps 8:9)

It is traditional to see David as the author of the Psalms. In fact, he is the recognised author of about 75 of the 150 psalms. Apart from this collection of 'Davidic Psalms' there are four other recognisable books of psalms: a group of psalms attributed to the family of Asaph, a group attributed to the sons of Korah, psalms of ascent to the Temple, and finally psalms of praise, or the "Great Hallel" psalms.

The Bible – and especially the Book of Psalms – has been the staple diet of Christians from the beginning. In the first centuries of Christian monasticism, the first task that a young novice was given was to memorise the New Testament and the Psalms. This was a way of shaping the soul of the novice and providing the young monk with an armoury of texts which could be used in prayer or reflected on while the novice or monk was doing manual labour.

Evagrius of Pontus wrote a book called *Antirrheticos*, which is a collection of hundreds of 'words' from the Scriptures that could be used to refute the demon's temptations. This method of using Scripture in the spiritual struggle was what Jesus used in his temptation in the desert. (Matthew 4: 1–17) Still today, in places like Mount Athos, there are reputed to be monks who know most of the Bible by heart.

John Cassian has a quaint way of describing the progress of a monk with regard to the Bible. He compares the novice to a "spiritual hedgehog" and the more advanced monk to the "agile and reasoning deer". (*Conferences* 10.11.2–4) The novice, like the timid hedgehog, seeks protection from the world by hiding behind the rock of the Gospel. The proficient monk, on the other hand, is like the deer which roams freely in the high pasturelands, taking in the words of the prophets and apostles. The novice needs to be careful to guard himself against the enemy. While this always remains the challenge for an advanced monk, nevertheless he has learned quickness of mind and the art of discernment.

But for both the novice and the advanced monk, the psalms were not something external, something simply to be read or sung. The masters of the Scriptures were all unanimous in urging that the young monk or novice should get behind and beyond the text to the "feeling of the text" that generated the psalms – whether praise, or joy, or anger, or loneliness, or disillusionment or praise or exaltation.

Even a quick glance through the collection of Psalms reveals how rich they are in images. In the Psalms we meet a woman with a child at the breast, a mother bird feeding her young, a man of integrity, a king on the throne, a man of sorrows, an archer, a person despised, a tender father, a faithful servant, a joyful singer, a harp player. We meet a lying witness, a flatterer, a fool. The psalmist's enemies are like vicious lions, fierce bulls, ravenous dogs who in the end become like chaff in the wind. The psalmist's God is like a shield, a rock, a mountain stronghold. This God's power is like a storm in a forest, a consuming fire, a clap of thunder splitting the rock. God leads the psalmist through trials that are like a storm at sea, a struggle against horses and chariots. The psalmist feels like a sheep lost in a thicket, a faithful person deserted by friends, a prisoner in chains, a sailor caught in a storm, someone drowning and as good as dead and finally someone saved from death. The bounty of God is like a sea teeming with fish, or a meadow sparkling with crops, or a field ripe with corn, or a cup brimming over with wine. Finally, the psalmist likens himself to a pilgrim on a journey, singing the joy-filled song, "Halleluia!"

Among all the images presented in the Psalms, one that especially draws our attention is the image of the desert. The desert was not only an image; it was a real experience for the Chosen People. When the Psalmist said that he felt like "a dry weary land without water" he was expressing an historical memory. He knew what living in a desert was like. He knew what the desert does to people. He knew what it was to feel hungry and especially what it was to feel the fierce pain of thirst.

THE DESERT

O God, you are my God, for you I long;
for you my soul is thirsting.
My body pines for you
like a dry, weary land without water.

Psalm 62:1

"No maps in this territory!"

For the people of the Old Testament, their experience of years of wandering in the desert was one of the most important aspects of their history. They looked back on this desert-time with both shame and nostalgia. The desert had exposed their disobedience, petulance and headstrong conduct. But it had also revealed God's forgiveness, tenderness, and closeness to them. In the desert God tested the people, instructed them and prepared them for the Promised Land. In the desert they were purified of their desire to turn back to the more comfortable way of life they had left behind; they were purified of their self-sufficiency, their self-seeking and their self-centredness and they were purified of the temptation to put their trust in gods other than the one God. But through these fires of purification, stripped of their comforts and support, wandering in a land of un-likeness, they began to understand that the God of Abraham and Moses was, after all, their rock, their refuge and their strength.

Centuries after the experience, Ezra the scribe recalled God's wonderful works in the desert. In his prayer, Ezra praised God for being so good to them:

> ".... You, so greatly loving, still did not forsake them in the wilderness: the pillar of cloud did not leave them that led them on their path by day, nor the pillar of fire by night, to light the way ahead of them by which they should go. You gave them your good spirit to make them wise, you did not withhold your manna from their mouths, you gave them water for their thirst. Forty years you cared for them in the wilderness: they went short of nothing, their clothes did not wear out, their feet were not swollen." [36]

People who go into the Sinai Desert are usually surprised at what they find. Contrary to their expectations, this desert isn't just a place of barrenness and emptiness with vast tracts of endless sand. It is also a place of incredible beauty, with huge rock mountains catching the early morning or evening light and reflecting it with magical effects. Watering holes and flowers appear in unexpected places. It is easy to see how their experience in the desert brought the Old Testament people closer to experiencing God's beauty, grandeur and providence.

Most of us don't need to go into any far-off country to find a desert. We have the desert imposed on us by the circumstances of our lives. The desert is more than a geographical spot: it is a condition, a state of soul. Deserts lie beneath the surface of our lives. They push through the controlled exterior of our lives from time to time, sometimes gradually, and sometimes in a single dramatic moment.

There are the ordinary deserts of daily routine which we sometimes want to avoid by compulsive activity or equally compulsive passivity, mindlessly staring at the television set or reaching for the change-channel button, anything to avoid what may be an opportunity to go a bit deeper into ourselves. There's the desert of loneliness which none of us wants to enter, but which imposes itself on us simply because we are unique human beings whose deepest longings can't be satisfied this side of eternity. There is the desert of meaninglessness which grips us when a sudden tragedy strikes us, when disappointment hits us or when we are betrayed by a trusted friend. We cry out: "Why should this happen to me?" "What's happening to me and my life?" We feel that life is gradually slipping out of control. Our guiding stars are fading. And we discover that there is no instant fix for these situations. The temptation we face is either to give up and throw it all away, or to try to control our lives by rigid attitudes, planning, organising and imposing our order on life. None of this works.

For many people, this is the threshold of the famous mid-life crisis. It may seem strange to turn to a fourth century desert-dweller for a description of a state that has only in recent years been recognised as part of the human condition. But that great psychologist of the spiritual life, Evagrius of Pontus, leaves us a striking picture of the state that he called *acedia*, the noon-day devil, that every monk of the desert faced sooner or later in his life. Imagine an earnest young monk who goes into the wilderness in search of God in solitude, and who soon discovers that the solitude that he thought would bring him most consolation is the very thing that terrifies him most. He is left with himself as his only companion. The day stretches out ahead of him, a day filled with – what?

Evagrius describes the situation:

> *"The demon of acedia, also called the noonday demon – is the one that causes the most serious trouble of all. He presses his attack upon the monk about the fourth hour and besieges the soul until the eighth hour. First of all he makes it seem that the sun barely moves, if at all, and that the day is fifty hours long. Then he constrains the monk to look constantly out of the windows, to walk outside the cell, to gaze carefully at the sun to determine how far it stands from the ninth hour, to look now this away and that to see if perhaps one of the brothers might be on the horizon. Then too he instils in the heart of the monk a hatred for the place, a hatred for his very life itself, a hatred for manual labour... This demon drives him along to desire other sites where he can more easily procure life's necessities, more readily find work and make a real success of himself... He depicts life stretching out for a long period of time and brings to the mind's eye the toil of the ascetic struggle and, as the saying goes, leaves no leaf unturned to induce the monk to forsake his cell and drop out of the fight."* [37]

It does not take much imagination on our part to let the centuries drop away and see how closely what is happening to this monk resembles what happens to us in the noon-day of our lives. The image of the sun's movement in the clear sky of the desert is a good image of human growth. In the morning the sun rises on a fresh day with signs of promise. As the sun rises the shadows shorten, the light increases, the heat becomes more intense. But at noon, just as the sun reaches its peak, the descent begins. And the descent of the sun means the reversal of all that has gone before. Shadows are cast in different directions. Heat which in the morning went outwards now seems to be withdrawn. The desert in the middle of the day is the hottest place on earth; in the evening it becomes bitterly cold. It's only a comparison, but it's no mere fantasy that makes us speak of the morning and spring of life, the noonday and summer of life and the evening and autumn of life.

In the middle of life we find ourselves at the threshold of a new moment, and many of us are unprepared for what this moment brings. We journey into this time of our lives with the false presumption that the truths and ideals that served us in the early part of life will continue to do so. But we can't live the afternoon of life with the same script we had for the morning. What was important in the morning will be unimportant in the evening. What was obscure in the morning will be clear in the evening. It can happen that convictions and principles which we held up till now begin to harden and grow increasingly rigid, or else they are discarded because they seem to be no longer relevant or useful to us.

As a male, I can only reflect on this experience as it affects many males. Sometimes this moment creeps up on us imperceptibly; at other times it hits us in a dramatic way. A man is at the height of his career, at a time of his greatest success. Suddenly he finds himself almost overwhelmed by restlessness. He experiences currents of deep melancholy or depression which he can't understand. Things go sour and dark. He hears himself making cynical or poisonous remarks about others. Life loses its spark. A persistent inner voice whispers in his ear: "What's the use of all this? What difference does your work – or you – make?"

We are familiar with the case of the man who at this moment throws away a successful career for something completely different, or who in his forties abandons his wife and family for what could only be described as a relationship based on pure fantasy.

One of the great enlightenments that hits us in the middle years is the realisation that there are whole areas of life which for various reasons we have so far avoided or resisted, especially the experiences of failure or weakness, of suffering, or of our physical reality, and in particular our sexuality. We have developed instinctive, knee-jerk mechanisms for avoiding these parts of life. Others may notice this in us, but we are often unconscious of it – till this moment, when the mid-life sun casts no shadows and we have no place to hide. Then truly we feel like "a dry weary land with no water".

Now the challenge faces us. We can either take the risk of standing firm in our desert, or we can try to construct make-shift hiding places. Some don't take the risk and become hypochondriacs, workaholics, applauders of the past, or eternal adolescents – all lamentable substitutes for what can become a moment of illumination. Those who take the risk of staying in the desert know that it could cost them their lives. Yet instinctively they know that the only life-giving solution is to stand firm and to go inward.

This moment is not only a recognised psychological stage in life. It is also a profoundly spiritual moment. It is in this moment that we might be able to renounce our idolatry, to break the false images we have of ourselves or of our God, and to discover our true selves and the true God.

When I think of those epic poems of heroic journeys into forests or across vast oceans or into searing deserts, I'm struck by the number of such stories that introduce a woman who accompanies the male hero. In *The Divine Comedy*, Dante meets Beatrice, who eventually guides him to the Blessed Virgin, and then to heaven. In the Grail legend Parsifal meets Blanche Fleur who brings him to understand himself. Even in the stories of the Desert Fathers and Mothers, the great saint Mary of Egypt meets the monk Zozima, and this relationship brings healing to them both.

Is there a lesson for us men here? The epic legends tell us that the hero needs the guidance of a woman in the significant stages of his journey. Maybe the desert experience in our inner lives might be just the moment when we men find a way of making friends with what people call the "feminine principle" in us. We are fascinated by this element in our psyche, and we are drawn to it; and yet somehow it frightens us. But we would do well to let the inner woman accompany us through the desert moments of life. Failure to do so produces all those attitudes of homophobia, lust for power, or bullying, which we instinctively know are travesties of true masculinity. The inner woman will not be silenced. She will either help us to become truly wise men, or she will become a witch, a trickster, impelling us to manipulate or deceive others. Or worse still, we will find that we have come to the evening of life constantly complaining about everything.

Anonymous Author

ow does one write biographical notes about some-one who is anonymous? The task is less difficult in this case than may at first appear. The image of the cloud comes from the pen of a fourteenth century English writer, about whom we can discover a lot, even if we will never know his name.

The writer was a contemporary of Julian of Norwich and those other mystics of the English tradition: Richard Rolle, Walter Hilton and Margery Kempe. The context of his life was the same as theirs: the Church divided by a papacy in conflict, England torn by the Peasants' Revolt of 1381, Europe ravaged by the Black Death and by the Hundred Years' War between the English and the French, civilisation itself on the verge of a dramatic turn.

The Black Death, which had reached Europe from the Crimea towards the end of 1347, raged through all the countries of Europe for three years, killing at least a third, and in some places up to half of the population. The great Italian poet Petrarch lived through these times and saw his wife, his son, his grandson and many of his friends struck down by the Black Death. He could hardly be blamed for thinking that his world might be at an end.

"When will posterity believe that there was a time when, without combustion of heaven or earth, without war or other visible calamity, not just this or that country, but almost the whole earth was left uninhabited.... Empty houses, deserted cities, unkempt fields, ground crowded with corpses, everywhere a vast and dreadful silence?" [40]

Such events – war, plague, famine, religious controversies – can inevitably breed in people an apocalyptic view of life and a sense that the end-times have arrived. The line between faith and superstition becomes blurred; a fascination for religious phenomena increases, and frequently this gives rise to mystical experiences both genuine and inauthentic.

This is the climate in which the anonymous author of *The Cloud of Unknowing* lived. Historians agree that he was most likely a monk, perhaps a Carthusian monk, who lived in either the Midlands of England or in Norfolk. Although it seems he was writing for a young novice, his language was not the Latin of the official Church theology, but Middle English, the language of the common people, and his advice is so practical and his style of writing is so clear and lucid that its teaching could be followed by anyone. This book has been called one of the greatest works of English spiritual teaching, and it is one that really needs to be read for itself.

From the beginning, the author makes it clear that he is writing for a simple and sincere person who wants to take up the spiritual journey. He is not writing for people who want extraordinary spiritual experiences, or for those who claim they have had such experiences. He is aware that there are people who wish to be up with the latest fad, or who flit from one latest book to another – even in fourteenth century England. These, he says clearly, are not the sort of people he is writing for. Look at what he says in the Introduction to the book:

"It doesn't matter whether the book belongs to you, or whether you are keeping it for someone else; whether you are taking it to someone, or borrowing it; you are not to read it, write or speak of it, nor allow another to do so, unless you really believe he is a person deeply committed to follow Christ perfectly."

"Moreover, I charge you, if you give this book to someone else, warn them (as I warn you) to take time to read it thoroughly. For it is very possible that certain chapters need the explanation given in other chapters to complete their meaning. As for worldly gossips, flatterers, the scrupulous, talebearers, and busybodies, I would just as soon they never laid eyes on this book. I had no intention of writing for them, and I prefer that they do not meddle with it."

The author is obviously a sharp-eyed observer of human nature who has a keen sense of humour. He hasn't kept his eyes cast down in his monastery chapel. He's noticed the odd behaviours of some of his monks, and he warns his young pupil against the pseudo-contemplatives he had seen in the monasteries:

"If their eyes are open, they are apt to be staring blankly like a madman, or peering like men who saw the devil, and well they might, for he is not far from them. Sometimes their eyes look like the eyes of wounded sheep near death. Some will let their heads drop to one side, as if a worm were in their ears. Others, like ghosts, utter shrill piping sounds that are supposed to pass for speech."

But for all the directness of his writing, the author is gentle and moderate, and he urges his disciple to develop these same two qualities: "Keep to the middle path: avoid the extremes", "Guard against too much or too little" in everything. This perhaps is why his book speaks to Christians of all types.

The author concludes his book with a statement that is a masterpiece of modesty:

"Should it seem that the way of prayer I have described in this book is unsuited to you spiritually or temperamentally, feel perfectly free to leave it aside and with wise counsel seek another in full confidence. In that case, I trust you hold me excused for all I have written here. Truly, I wrote only according to my simple understanding of these things and with no other purpose than that of helping you. So read this book over two or three times. The more often you read it the better, for that much more shall you grasp its meaning."

It's worth reading the book. The writer's teaching is as practical for today as it was in the fourteenth century.

THE DESERT

*This is what you are to do: lift your heart up to the Lord, and
with a gentle stirring of love desiring him for his own sake and
not for his gifts. Diligently persevere until you feel joy in this. For
in the beginning it is usual to feel nothing but a kind of darkness
about your mind, or as it were a cloud of unknowing. You will
seem to know nothing and to feel nothing except a naked intent
toward God in the depths of your being. Try as you might, this
darkness and this cloud will remain between you and your God.
But learn to be at home in this darkness. For if, in this life, you
hope to feel and see God as He is in Himself, it must be within
this darkness and this cloud.*

The Cloud of Unknowing, Chapter 3

"Pierce the Cloud with a sharp dart"

From the very beginning, the friends of God have understood that their journey to God rested on two truths, spelled out in the Letter to the Hebrews: "Anyone who comes to God must believe that He exists and that He rewards those who search for Him." [39]

Those who search for God must first of all believe that God exists. But more than that, they must believe that God is more keen to be found than we are to find. Certainly, more keen to be found than we could ever imagine.

Simple as it may seem, behind this statement lies the whole sweep of the teaching of the mystics on prayer. There's a paradox here: God is *God*, but God became a *human being* for our sake. To approach God is to approach the supreme being, infinitely holy and beyond us; yet infinitely near to us because God became flesh in Jesus Christ, and because this same God lives in us through the power of the Holy Spirit. "Closer is he than breathing; nearer than hands or feet" wrote the poet Tennyson.[40] These two features, the "transcendence" (distance) of God and the "immanence" (closeness) of God must always find a place – and will always cause a tension – in Christian spirituality.

The question has always been: how can we reach communion with a God who is God, and yet has become one of us and is within us as the one in whom "we live and move and have our being?" [41]

In time, two "schools" of thought developed, and these have been, and still are, two different approaches to the life of prayer. One school of thought says that God is experienced as "light": a radiance, a clear intellectual insight, an understanding. This school of thought came to be called the "Way of Light" or in Latin the "*via positiva*", and in Greek the "*kataphatic*" way. Walter Hilton, a contemporary of Julian of Norwich belongs to this school. In his book *The Ladder of Perfection* he writes:

"But the aye (ever) lasting love of Jhesu is a true day and blessed light. For God is both love and light, and He is aye lasting, as Saint John saith ... He that loveth God dwelleth all in light. Then what man perceiveth and seeth the love of this world false and failing, and for this he will forsake it and seek the love of God; he may not at once feel the love of Him, but he must abide awhile in the night, for he may not suddenly come from that one light to that other, that is, from the love of the world to perfect love of God. This night is nought else but a forebearing and a withdrawing of the soul from all earthly things, by a great desire and yearning for to love and see and seek Jhesu and all ghostly (spiritual) things." [42]

The other school of thought says that God can only be known in "darkness". God, being God, cannot be reached through symbols or images, and should not be reached by thought or imagination. All that we can say of God is that God is *"not*-this" or *"not*- that". This school of thought was called the "Way of Darkness" or in Latin the *"via negativa,"* and in Greek the *"apophatic"* way.

In some of St Augustine's writings this apophatic tradition is evident:

"God is inexpressible. It is easier for us to say what God is not than what God is...Nothing is comparable to him. If you could conceive of him you would conceive of something other than God. He is not at all what you have conceived him to be."

Interestingly, both the apophatic and the kataphatic schools of thought drew confirmation for their teaching from the Scriptures, and from the same book of the Bible. "The Way of Light" cites chapter 24 of the Book of Exodus, where the author speaks of Moses, Aaron, Nadab and Abihu going up to the mountain of God:

"They saw the God of Israel,
they gazed on God.
They ate and they drank." [43]

Moses and *his* companions experienced God in a direct way, seeing and gazing on God, enjoying God's hospitality.

On the other hand, the followers of the Way of Darkness refer to Chapter 19 of the same book of the Bible, where the author speaks of "thunder on the mountain, and lightning flashes, and a dense cloud" into which Moses entered, while all the people trembled at the base of the mountain:

> *"The Mountain of Sinai was entirely*
> *wrapped in smoke;*
> *Yahweh called Moses to the top of the mountain*
> *and Moses went up, right into the cloud."* [44]

These two schools of "darkness" and "light" are complementary rather than exclusive of each other. The darkness that people experience is actually the experience of entering into a light that's too great for us to cope with. If one looks directly into the sun, one becomes blinded by the light. In trying to explain this paradox, St Symeon the New Theologian, uses the image of a person entering into the sea:

> *"While a man standing on the seashore is on dry land, he can see*
> *around him and encompass with his eyes the expanse of the sea. But*
> *if he begins to wade into the waters and to plunge into them, the*
> *more deeply he enters the less he sees what is outside. So it is with the*
> *participants of Divine light. The greater the knowledge of God they*
> *attain, the greater, correspondingly, becomes their lack of knowledge*
> *(of everything outside God.)"* [45]

The experience of light brings about a sense of darkness, and the darkness leads us into light.

One of the great masters of this Way of Darkness was the mysterious but highly influential sixth century writer, Dionysius the Areopagite or Pseudo-Dionysius. Two mystical works are attributed to Dionysius: *The Mystical Theology* and *The Divine Names*. Dionysius chooses the word "darkness" as the most appropriate way to describe God. But he combines this word with "light" to form a sort of contradictory description, and in this way he conveys the mystery and the paradox of God. He writes of God as "brilliant darkness", or "darkness so far above light", and "darkness concealed from all light". God lies "beyond all vision and knowledge". On the other hand, there is an element of "light" in God. God is light because we can know God; God is darkness because we cannot know God. It is as simple and as complex as that.

The writings of Dionysius had a marked influence on later writers like Meister Eckhart, John Tauler, Henry Suso and clearly on John of the Cross.

The author of *The Cloud of Unknowing* belongs within this school of thought. What he puts before his young pupil goes something like this: In love, God is calling the young disciple to a new stage in the spiritual journey. This will demand of him a longing desire and a deep love for God. It will involve spiritual watchfulness, forgetting the past, and a determination to reach God through love.

The author describes this way of reaching God, using the image of a cloud. Between the disciple and God there is a great cloud, a "cloud of unknowing". This cloud of unknowing exists because God cannot be put into our minds. We cannot grasp God through intellectual processes. We cannot know or understand God as we can understand and know factual matters. God is hidden from us by this cloud of unknowing. The only way to pierce through the cloud is by love.

So, the author advises his disciple to stand beneath the cloud of unknowing and as it were fire "sharp darts of longing love" which will penetrate that cloud:

> *"Let your longing relentlessly beat upon the cloud of unknowing*
> *that lies between you and your God.*
> *Pierce that cloud with the sharp dart of longing love.*
> *Spurn the thought of anything less than God,*
> *and do not give up this work for anything."*

Once this love has sprung, the disciple can "press" longingly upon God. Love is the key to contemplation. God is not known through thought, but through love. In his marvellous medieval English style, the author writes: "By love may he be gotten and holden, but by thought never." Love is the beginning and the end of the spiritual journey. There is no thinking at this stage. Even thoughts about God are a distraction. The author advises his pupil that in his attempt to "pierce the cloud with sharp darts of longing love" he should use short prayers. "A short prayer pierces the heavens," he writes. The disciple shouldn't spend time composing fine speeches. Just a word or a phrase is enough. Words like "Love!" "Mercy!" "Jesus!" will pierce the cloud if they are inspired by love.

The author goes on to explain that just as a cloud of unknowing stands between the disciple and God, the disciple needs to construct another cloud – a cloud of forgetting – under which he puts all his thoughts or considerations. The disciple stands midway between these two clouds: the cloud of unknowing which conceals God, and the cloud of forgetting which conceals his thoughts, memories and distractions.

Even though this little book was written seven centuries ago for a contemplative monk, it is amazingly relevant for those of us who live busy lives in the twenty-first century. When asked, most people would say that they experience God sometimes in a *kataphatic* way of light, but most often in the *apophatic* way of darkness. Many of us experience the 'darkness' of God more frequently than the 'light' of God.

I've read many books on prayer and spirituality. Many of them present the experience of God in a way that I don't easily identify with. For me, and I suspect for most of us, prayer will be an experience of obscurity. Many of us in times of prayer find that our minds are filled with distractions darting about like monkeys in the trees. The most we can do is to fire short prayers up to God as we lurch from one life-crisis to another. "Help!" or "Mercy!" or "Lord save us!" sometimes are the most we can say when it comes to prayer.

We can all take heart. There's a very strong tradition, beginning with Jesus himself, that tells us that the state of interior darkness is not uncommon, and that this sort of short prayer is often the most authentic prayer we can make. When the writings of Mother Teresa of Calcutta were published, many people were surprised to learn that this smiling worker for the poor had spent most of her life in total interior darkness of spirit. God calls many of us to enter into a darkness, which seems to obscure any felt experience of God, but which like the cloud over Mount Sinai reveals God waiting for us with love.

At the same time, it is important to take note of the other cloud the author speaks of: the cloud of forgetting. There are many unwelcome and unsavoury guests residing in our memories and imaginations. Real or imagined hurts, memories of lustful experiences and imaginings of a better life make their presence felt when we try to sit still. We make speeches in our minds to those who have hurt us, or to the world itself, which never seems to understand or value us. These things, the author says, need to be shown the door of our minds and hearts and asked quietly to leave. It's no good firing those sharp darts of longing love through the cloud of unknowing unless we have put those other thoughts in their place underneath a cloud of forgetting.

This great fourteenth century spiritual master teaches us that the "work" of prayer is really God working in us. We make ourselves ready, we sharpen our desire, we frame those desires in short words that come from the heart, and we leave the rest to God.

Diadochus of Photike

he fourth and fifth centuries were centuries of intense theological discussion, debate and controversy. In those two centuries, four of the first seven Ecumenical Councils of the Church took place. These councils dealt especially with questions that were fundamental to Christian belief: how can God be one and yet three Persons? How can Jesus be God and man; and if he is God and man, is Mary to be called Mother of Jesus only, or Mother of God?

These are not purely speculative and theoretical questions. Our behaviour as Christians depends on our beliefs about God and Jesus. And the way we pray depends on this as well. Do Christians, for example, pray to a God who has human features? Do they try to imagine God as they pray? Or do they try to rid themselves of all thoughts and keep their minds empty? Where does prayer take place – in one's head, or in one's heart, or somewhere else?

This last question exercised the reflections of many people from the beginning, as it still does today. People beginning to pray are often not quite sure how they might best develop their relationship with God in prayer. They often ask, "What am I supposed to do when I pray? Do I simply recite prayers? Or am I supposed to think about things? Should my prayer be based on remembering and reflecting on stories of Jesus? Is it good or bad to have feelings about God when I'm praying?"

In those early centuries, several different positions were taken, some of them at seemingly opposite extremes. At one extreme were those who taught that prayer took place in the mind, and in a mind that was empty of all thoughts, memories, imaginings or human reasonings. At another extreme were those who taught that prayer takes place in a person's affective or feeling faculties. They proposed a spiritualised approach to counter what was claimed to be an extreme intellectualist approach.

An example of this extreme spiritualised approach was the Messalian heresy, which emerged from Asia Minor in the fourth century. The Messalanians, whose name derives from the Syriac word for prayer, endeavoured to find a way of following St Paul's exhortation to "pray without ceasing". According to their teaching, when one who prays has driven out the demons within, he or she is rendered impervious to sin no matter what happens.

Both the extreme form of intellectualism and the Messalian doctrine were condemned by Church councils. Unfortunately the two extremes have been attributed by some, however wrongly, to Evagrius of Pontus and to Macarius of Egypt, with Evagrius being credited with the intellectualist approach and Macarius with the extreme affective approach.

As in everything, the truth is in the middle way, and a fifth century bishop in Greece by the name of Diadochus of Photike proposed such a middle way between the two extreme approaches. Diadochus understood and was deeply influenced by the teachings of both Evagrius and Macarius. His teaching holds the two approaches together and keeps them in balance.

Little is known of Diadochus' life, except that he was Bishop of Photike in Epirus in Greece and that he lived from 400 to 486. He described the experience of true prayer as an experience of the "mind" *and* the "heart". The effect of mankind's disobedience in the Garden of Eden was to lead our ancestors to lose the "memory of God" which was a feature of the state of paradise, and to wander in a "land of unlikeness" without the sense of God. But, according to Diadochus, we are able to regain our original state of "mindfulness of God" through the grace of God and through calling on the name of

Jesus. Diadochus is one of the first authorities on the Jesus Prayer, and one of the first to write about it.

When Diadochus uses the words "mind" (*nous*) or "heart" (*kardia*), he doesn't use them in the sense that we understand those words. The "mind" is more than human intelligence. It is the faculty of spiritual intelligence which enables us to see through the ordinary things and recognise the presence of God in everything. And the "heart" is more than our emotions or feelings. It is the centre of our being. Prayer, then, according to Diadochus, is an activity in which we bring our mind into our heart, and it is in that state that the Spirit of God touches us. This leads to one thing: *doxologia*. We cry out – as no other living creature can – "Glory to you, O God."

What makes Diadochus' teaching compelling is that he is not repeating hear-say knowledge. He knows from his own experience what he writes about, and more than once he says: "This is very important – know it for certain".

Diadochus' teaching on prayer is a good balance to any tendency to disconnect mind and heart in prayer. Some writers seem to encourage their disciples to make a journey of liberation from the head into the heart. "Get out of your head, with its dull and dry rationalising, and journey to the springs of living water in the heart", they seem to say. This sort of dualism is far removed from Diadochus and the ancient tradition of prayer. He opens the way to an understanding of prayer as "mind-in-the-heart", a way of praying that is very characteristic of later Russian spirituality:

> "The principal thing is to stand with the mind in the heart before God, and to go on standing before Him unceasingly day and night until the end of life." [46]

Diadochus was one of the great popularisers of Desert spirituality, and was regarded as the most important spiritual writer of his century. His writings influenced Maximus the Confessor, Simeon the New Theologian, Gregory of Palamas, and later the author of the Russian Classic text *The Way of the Pilgrim*. It is through the influence of this little book that many people of the West have come to be influenced by the teaching of Diadochus of Photike.

THE UNRUFFLED SEA

*Those who are engaged in spiritual warfare must always keep
their hearts tranquil. Only then can the mind sift the impulses it
receives and store in the treasure house of the memory those that
are good and come from God, while rejecting altogether those
that are perverse and devilish.*

*When the sea is calm, the fishermen's eyes can see the movements
of the fish deep down, so that hardly any of them can escape. But
when the sea is ruffled by the wind, the turmoil of the waves hides
from sight the creatures that would easily have been seen if the
sea wore the smile of calm. The skill of the fisherman is of little
use in rough weather.*

*Something of the same sort happens with the soul, especially
when it is stirred to the depths by anger.*

Diadochus of Photike, Spiritual works, 23

Making choices

Diadochus' image of the "unruffled sea" highlights two qualities which masters of the spiritual life, going right back to the first Christian centuries, have regarded as essential: tranquillity of soul, and insight or the capacity to make right choices.

Diadochus uses two Greek words to describe these attitudes: *apathaeia* and *diakrisis*.

The point of everything that the early Christian teachers called *ascesis* was to bring the deepest part of a person to a point of tranquility and focus. This state they called *apathaeia*. Players in an orchestra poised and watching the conductor's baton for the moment to begin to play; the rugby player poising himself before kicking a goal, calculating the strength and direction of the wind, focusing on the cross-bar; the high jumper concentrating on the bar before making the jump – all these are in something of the state of *apathaeia*, whether they know it or not. *Apathaeia* is about being alert and poised for action.

Evagrius of Pontus is a chief source for understanding the meaning of *apathaeia*. Before him, Ignatius of Antioch and Clement of Alexandria had used the term. For these early writers and their followers, *apathaeia* is a state of peaceful calm, free from anger and self-centred emotions, which enables us to observe in a truly clear-eyed fashion, first of all ourselves, and then others, and to do so with realism and compassion. *Apathaeia* frees us from the domination of our inner demons and gives us back to the power of God. It doesn't take away any of our natural human feelings. Rather, it purifies our feelings and takes away the things in us that are disordered, or which blur our vision of what is going on inside us.

Apathaeia is the condition for making good decisions, and it is also the fruit or the sign of a good decision having been made. It is a state of contained energy, and not at all like what our look-alike word "apathy" connotes. Over the centuries some people have made the mistake of misinterpreting the meaning of the Greek word.

Saint Jerome made this mistake. Jerome had no love for Evagrius and fiercely ridiculed and criticised him and other teachers of the East. He caricatured the idea of *apathaeia* by suggesting that Evagrius wanted to make human beings "either a stone or God". Unfortunately, the Western Church has tended to follow Jerome's views on this matter, and this has resulted in a suspicion of oriental thinking, whether Christian or otherwise. Even saints can be mischief-makers, and Jerome did the church a lot of harm through his acerbic writing. The true notion of *apathaeia* is far removed from the sort of caricature that Jerome portrayed.

This state doesn't come easily. It is the result of those attitudes we have already considered: *metanoia, skopos, telos, prosoch* and *nepsis*.

In the literature of the early church there are many examples of this state of *apathaeia* in the lives of Christian monks. A good example is found in the biography of St Antony of the Desert, written by St Athanasius. Athanasius reports how, after many years in a cave, locked away from human contact and struggling with his demons, Antony finally emerged from his cave. The people who witnessed the event were amazed at what they saw. Antony was neither too fat from lack of exercise, nor too thin from his ascetical life; he looked neither older nor younger than his years; he was neither worn out from his struggles with the demons, nor overjoyed at his triumph over them. Athanasius describes his exit from the cave. He emerged, "equal to himself, governed by reason, natural". (*Life of St Anthony*, 14) That state of interior and exterior tranquility is the state of *apathaeia*.

I found a more contemporary illustration of this state in the Norwegian Maritime Museum in Oslo. On display there was a striking painting by Norwegian artist Wilhelm Otto Peters (1851–1935). Called *Crab catchers*, it shows three young girls in a small boat, leaning over the side of the boat with lines into the water, catching crabs. The observer is drawn into the scene because a sense of intimacy is created by the absence of any horizon. What is more striking is that the girls in the boat are totally oblivious of the artist or anybody else watching. They are silent, intently gazing into the water which is still and unruffled, carefully observing any movement in the sea bed. The picture has a sense of intimacy, of silence and careful observation, of expectant waiting, of alertness to any movement that might indicate the presence of a crab.

This state of alertness and watchfulness is what Diadochus was describing in his image of the unruffled sea. You see below the surface of your life and you recognise what's going on there. You can see that – to use the classic spiritual jargon – there's some movement of the spirit going on. *Apathaeia* creates the conditions in which we can see what's under the surface of our lives.

But how do we know how to recognise whether this is a movement of the good spirit, or of the bad spirit, or whether it is simply our own psychological state or the states of depression or euphoria? How do we become able to say to these interior movements: "I know who you are: you are (or you are not) of God"?

The next state, implied in Diadochus' image is that of *diakrisis* or discernment. This is the gift of being able to recognise and either follow or dismiss the movements within us. In another part of his writings, Diadochus points out that the "inner senses" follow much the same pattern as our external senses. Our physical sense of taste, he says, leads us when we are healthy to distinguish unfailingly between good food and bad. In the same way, our intellect, when properly trained, can more easily recognise the good "movements" in our heart.

This is where his image is telling. A good fisherman knows how to be crafty, and how to resist the temptation to take the first nibble on the line. The good angler knows when to wait for the big fish, and how to recognise it when it comes. *Diakrisis* or discernment is something like that. The gift of discernment enables us to know what among our subterranean motives is pure and worth pursuing, and what should be cast aside as springing from self-seeking or self-delusion. But this discernment can only take place when the state of inner tranquility is established.

This gift of *diakrisis* or discernment is a gift of the Holy Spirit and can't be acquired by our own engineering or efforts. But we can dispose ourselves to receive the gift if it is to be given to us by the Spirit.

A striking example of *apathaeia* and *diakrisis* in action can be found in the *Acts of the Apostles*. This is an account of the first Council of the Church held in Jerusalem around the year 50 AD. The council was called to resolve a problem which was of utmost importance to the Jews. If the Way of Jesus was the fulfillment of the Jewish law and practice, then should pagans become Jews before they became Christians? And what were

Jewish converts to do about ceremonial practices like circumcision, which according to the Jewish law was essential for salvation, abstaining from blood-meat, and other religious practices? This was a topic that aroused great emotions. It was the topic on which Paul openly opposed Peter and shamed him for jumping from one side of the argument to the other. The elders were summoned to discuss and resolve the matter. The whole story is related in chapter 15 of the Acts of the Apostles.

First, the account tells us: "there was much discussion". Then, Peter got up and addressed the assembly, telling them of his personal experience. Next, the author tells us that "the whole assembly fell silent" as Paul and Barnabas shared their experiences. James spoke next. When he had finished, the assembly made a decision. So sure were they that they had listened and discerned carefully that they were able to write to the Christians scattered in different places that the final outcome had been decided "by the Holy Spirit and by us". (Acts 15:26)

In an age where discussion is reduced to a shouting match between two or more people trying to convince the other of their views; when what is called dialogue amounts to two or more people talking at the same time; when silence in debate is simply a pause in word flow and a chance for the protagonists to draw breath, this attitude of "falling silent" as another speaks, of listening carefully to the experience of others, is truly counter-cultural. When our means of social communication enable us to send out any ill-considered ideas instantly and to anywhere in the world, we desperately need to develop the art of seeking space and quiet where we can look into our inner motives, to recognise what's going on inside, and what forces drive our actions. Stimulated by over-choice and lots of noise, it's difficult – but essential – to find some space where one can be truly quiet and at enough peace to make considered choices.

Possibly because he could see the effect of Jerome's bitter criticism of Evagrius' use of the word *apathaeia*, when John Cassian introduced this Eastern insight to the West, he gave it the Latin title *puritas cordis*, or "purity of heart". Even that title is subject to misinterpretation, but Wilhelm Otto Peters' painting adds colour to Diadochus' image and captures something of the inner and outer stillness, the focus and the single-minded concentration involved in making a decision that "seems good to the Holy Spirit".

Nicodemus of the Holy Mountain

 icodemus of the Holy Mountain belongs to the Greek Orthodox tradition, and that gives a clue to understanding his name. He was a monk who lived on Mount Athos, known to all Orthodox as the "Holy Mountain". For Orthodox Christians, Mount Athos is a symbol and a reference point of faith. For over 1,000 years, monks – and only monks – have lived on this isthmus extending out into the Aegean Sea from the north of Greece, near Thessaloniki. There are 20 large monasteries on the promontory, along with many smaller monasteries and houses. Some monks live in the large monasteries, some live in the smaller monasteries and some live in even smaller communities of two or three monks. Some live entirely on their own as hermits.

During the 1,100 years of its existence this sacred place has known moments of intense religious fervour, times of collapse and times of reform. Monasteries have been pillaged by marauders and looters, destroyed by fire and earthquake and rebuilt again. At its peak, according to historians, there were estimated to be more than 30,000 monks on the land. At its lowest point, there were about 1,400.

One of the lowest points in its history was in the early 1960s. In 1963, the year of the celebration of the 1,000th year of the monastic foundation, there was cause for celebration and speech-making. But in the speeches there was already a hint of a troubling question: had this great spiritual centre run its course, and was it time to close all the huge but barely-inhabited monasteries on the isthmus?

The question was never pursued. A turnaround was in sight, and since 1969 there has been a remarkable flourishing of monastic life on the Holy Mountain. Large numbers of young, black-bearded, educated men have become monks. Each year thousands of pilgrims, seekers and tourists come to visit the monasteries. They spend no more than three nights in one or other of the monasteries before returning home, renewed by their contact with the Holy Mountain and its monks.

There have been other great periods of revival on Mount Athos. One of these took place in the second half of the eighteenth century. Three centuries earlier, in 1453, the Ottoman Turks sacked Constantinople and brought an end to the Byzantine Empire, which had ruled most of the Greek-speaking world for more than 1,100 years. From 1453 until the Greek War of Independence in 1829, all of Greece lay under the rule of the Ottoman Turks. Mount Athos alone remained independent, but the monks needed to protect their spiritual independence by adopting a defensive attitude to outside influences. This led to a form of rigid traditionalism. In their struggles to ensure that they remained faithful to their spiritual heritage, they were not able to develop it in a creative way.

But in the second half of the eighteenth century, a spiritual renaissance took place. This revival was set in motion by a group of monks from Mount Athos who believed that the regeneration of the Greek nation would come through a return to the sources of their spirituality: the Fathers of the Church. This movement was not an inflexible, literal or blind re-statement of the past. It was a creative attempt to unearth the roots of Christian faith as enshrined especially in the spiritual tradition of the East. The practice of prayer, rooted in the tradition of the Desert Fathers and Mothers and developed through experience and reform, was a major feature of this revival on Mount Athos.

Two personalities were at the heart of the revival: Macarius of Corinth (1731–1805) and Nicodemus of the Holy Mountain (1749–1809).

Born on the island of Naxos in 1749, Nicodemus was given a broad education. He was blessed with a remarkable memory. A contemporary wrote that "he knew from memory whatever he read, not only the phil-osophical, economic, medical, astronomic and even military treatises which he read, but also all the poets, and the historians ancient and new, Greek and Latin, as well as all the writings of the Fathers. It was enough for him to read a book once and remember it throughout his life." [47]

He was drawn to the monastic life and in 1775 he went to Mount Athos and entered the monastery of Diiou. Nicodemus was strong-ly Orthodox in his faith, but he was also interested in and open to the tradition of the West. He translated the *Spiritual Exercises* of St Ignatius of Loyola and the *Spiritual Combat* of Lorenzo Scupoli into Greek for the use of Orthodox Christians.

It was while he was on Athos that he and Macarius of Corinth embarked on a work of compiling a book of texts on prayer and the spiritual life. The two compilers gathered together texts dating from the fourth and the fifteenth centuries on the ascetical life and in particular on the experience of prayer. These texts draw from the experience of the Desert Fathers, the mystical writers of Mt Sinai and Syria, and some of the Greek Fathers. The title of the book, *Philokalia*, means "love of beauty" – love, in particular, of God as the source of all things beautiful. This huge anthology has had a vast readership in the Church of the East, and it has remained a funda-mental source of enlightenment and instruction for the Orthodox believers, second only to the Bible.

St Nicodemus described the *Philokalia* as "a mystical school of inward prayer". It is a remarkable anthology, not at all easy to work through, but rewarding. It had a profound effect on the author of the famous little Russian spiritual classic, *The Way of a Pilgrim*. The pilgrim writes: "As I began to put it into practice I tasted a sweetness I could not even have imagined until now. Often I spent an entire day sitting in the forest carefully reading the *Philokalia* and learning many wondrous things from it. My heart burned with a desire for union with God through interior prayer."

TINY CREATURES IN THE MUD

The passions can be likened to certain tiny creatures found in the mud at the bottom of a lake. As long as they do not have anything to eat they are content to lie there in peace. But as soon as food is put into the water, you can see them immediately moving and rising up from the depth to get the food. In the same manner the passions remain peacefully within the heart as long as they do not receive from the outside through the senses, any nourishment and pleasure. But as soon as such a pleasure enters, especially through the eyes, these passions move directly toward the desirable nourishment.

St Nicodemus of the Holy Mountain, Philokalia

"It depends on what you feed"

One of Victor Hugo's stories tells of a terrifying incident on board a ship caught in a storm at sea. As the storm rages around the frail vessel, the sailors hear a noise and feel a thud coming from inside the vessel. It is a noise quite unlike any other sound. Instinctively the sailors know what it is: one of the cannons on the ship, weighing twenty-four pounds, has broken loose. This is the most dangerous accident that can possibly take place on board ship, Hugo writes. Nothing more terrible can happen to a sloop of war in open sea and under full sail.

The sailors go below, terror written on their faces. They now face a double danger. Not only are they threatened by the external forces of the storm raging outside, they are now threatened by dangers inside the ship. They know the danger the cannon presents to the safety of the ship and to everyone on board. They know that the cannon can't be left to roam free inside the ship. Yet they know, too, that the solution is not to throw it overboard. The only solution is to keep it in its place. Finally they manage to chain the loose cannon back in place, and the ship is saved.

Nicodemus of the Holy Mountain would have understood exactly what Victor Hugo was getting at in this parable of human life. There's a loose cannon in all of us, threatening to break us down. Nicodemus is thoroughly steeped in the ancient tradition of the Desert. He is able to offer a kind of psycho-spiritual understanding of what happens inside the Christian pilgrim. It is as if this centuries-old tradition can put into our hands a user's manual and a kit of tools to help us understand and deal with the inner workings of our human psyche.

The user's manual evolved through the wisdom of the guides and teachers of the Desert tradition. It became clear to these insightful men and women that there are four things that beset people who make the journey inwards. They called these things "demons", "things", "passions" and "thoughts". They didn't imagine "demons" as we might think they did. Demons are simply those things that seem to come at us and catch us unaware, making us do or say things that go against our better nature. "Things" are the events or the circumstances that have shaped our lives: our parentage, our family life, our upbringing, the political situation of the country in which we live and other external happenings.

None of these four things has absolute power over us. They can all be handled, but they each need different treatment, a different set of tools. What the Desert tradition calls demons and things are outside ourselves. They can be dealt with or avoided by moving away from the point of trouble or irritation.

The other two realities – passions and thoughts – are much more significant because they are within us, they remain with us, and we take them with us wherever we go.

We all know what passions are, and soon the Desert guides began to enumerate them, most particularly anger, lust, greed and pride. These are permanent fixtures in our lives. They lie there, dormant or otherwise, and like the cannon in Victor Hugo's story, they have potential for destruction, either by firing off or by rattling round and breaking down our inner fabric. Nicodemus described the passions as the creatures in the mud waiting to be fed.

But Evagrius of Pontus had another insight which is particularly relevant, and it concerned what he believed were the things that triggered the passions. These things he called "thoughts", or in Greek *logismoi*. In Evagrius' terminology the "thoughts" were just that – thoughts. They were neither good nor bad, though they were closely connected to the passions and could easily stir them up. Evagrius numbered eight of these *logismoi*: gluttony, lust, avarice, sadness, anger, listlessness, vainglory and pride. These names are familiar to us as what we have come to call the "seven deadly sins". But Evagrius didn't see them as already moral faults. The *logismoi* were not already sins or passions, even though they could easily be a step in that direction. They were more like obsessive and compulsive ideas, and they couldn't easily be talked down. Their constant companion was self-deception.

For example, the *logismos* of gluttony was not in fact over-eating or gorging oneself on fine foods. It was the thought that often beset a monk in the desert, that he may injure his health by his fasting and ascetical practices. What would happen if he got sick? Would it not be wise to set some extra medicine aside just in case it may be needed at some future time? The *logismos* of lust was not necessarily actual sexual misdemeanour, but a recurring fear in the monk's mind that there may be no one to care for him in his old age. Or it may be a memory of his past life which he entertains and embellishes with his fertile imagination. The thought of human companionship becomes more attractive to him than the vocation he has taken up. The *logismos* of sadness was not actual depression or melancholy, but a sort of creeping nostalgia for what the monk had in the past, a temptation to look on the past as a sort of golden time in his life. The *logismos* of anger was something much more subtle than actually being angry with someone. It was the recurring thought of grievances done by someone to the monk, the constant speeches that the monk made in his mind when he was alone.

The ultimate effect of these *logismoi* or "thoughts" was to blunt the edge of the monk's commitment to his vocation; they would lead to actions or behaviours incompatible with his life as a monk, eventually making him think about leaving the desert and returning to his former life.

Isaac the Syrian in the seventh century describes some of these "thoughts" in words that sound quite contemporary.

> *"These trials are the following: laziness, heaviness in the body, despondency, confusion of thoughts, anxiety caused by exhaustion, temporary loss of hope, dark thoughts, constant presence of a lustful thought, quick temper, desire to have everything one's own way, to argue, to reprimand others, absurd and laughable suspicions that they are scorned by people, and finally the desire to talk endlessly and chatter senselessly."*

Isaac's list is interesting: heaviness of body, physical exhaustion, loss of hope, suspicions about other people's intentions, and compulsive talking form a sort of seed-bed for what might grow into full-blown passions which can eventually overpower us.

I find something very realistic about this teaching. The terminology may belong to another time, but the reality these writers describe is absolutely contemporary. My world may not be that of the desert wastes of Egypt or Syria, but I know what it is to be beset by those obsessive fears and concerns about the future, or those constantly returning memories of hurts inflicted by others, of injustices done or words that have left a wound. I know what it is to find myself making speeches to others in my mind when it is not occupied by other things. I know what it is to want to be – or think that I actually am – someone other than what I am. I know what it is to have a higher opinion of myself than is warranted, or even worse, to have a lower opinion of myself than I should have. The things that lead us to obsessive concern about appearances, to excessive care for the body or irresponsible neglect of it; the whisperings that tell us that we are entitled to put ourselves first at all times, or that we can find a good way of seeking revenge for wrongs done to us-- all these are all what our Desert ancestors called "thoughts". There is no running away from these things, because they are within us. And they have the potential to make us less than what we could be. They are a step towards the passions that Nicodemus talks of in his image.

The Desert tradition has given us two tools for handling these *logismoi*, and once again Evagrius of Pontus is the spokesperson for this tradition.

In the first way, Evagrius proposes that we use the strategy used by Jesus in his temptations in the desert. To the demon's trick of using Scripture to support his temptations, Jesus answered back with another text from Scripture. This technique of "answering back" (in Greek *antirrhēsis*), is proposed by Evagrius as a tool for fighting the besetting thought. Evagrius wrote a book, entitled *Antirrhētikos*, in which he gathered 498 Scripture passages that could be used to answer back to the *logismoi*.[48]

For example, Evagrius proposes: "Against the thought that entices me to nostalgia for my city, my family, my loved ones: For here we have no lasting city, but we are looking for the city that is to come" (Heb 13:14); or "Against the thoughts that due to listlessness dare to complain: Do not complain as some of them did, and were destroyed by the destroyer" (1 Cor 10:10); or "Against the thought that is anxious about food and drink and tries to accumulate them: Cast your anxiety upon the Lord, and he will sustain you." (Ps 54:23)

Evagrius offers a second tool: observe the thoughts. Don't resist them, he says, but don't judge them either. Just observe them carefully. Note when these thoughts arise, what sorts of things arouse them, what sort of mood they come from or what sort of mood they produce in us. He asks us to observe how long these thoughts last, and what happens when we give them space. One's spiritual father or *abba* will be able to guide us from here on.

Whatever tool one uses with these thoughts, there is one un-changeable rule: Don't interact with them! Don't give them the time of day. Once a person enters into dialogue with the *logismos,* the battle is lost. The debate never goes in favour of the person. Soon the thought has its own life and becomes an action. And furthermore, once the thought has been entertained it takes up residence and is not easy to eject.

This sort of self-examination is not at all self-preoccupation or self-indulgence. Rather, it's an attempt at being fundamentally realistic.

People sometimes suggest that the modern person has lost a sense of sin. Maybe, but maybe not. Perhaps what we have lost is not so much the sense of sin, but the awareness of where sin lies. Those of us who belong to a Christian tradition that offers sacramental confession have at our disposal a wonderful instrument for cleaning the glass of our perception and understanding where those *logismoi* are at work. Sadly, my pastoral experience tells me that the great possibilities contained in the sacrament are scarcely realised. What for many people could be a moment for owning the truth about oneself becomes paradoxically a moment of disowning that truth. It becomes a way of naming particular actions without looking closely at the roots of those actions, those tiny creatures in the mud of our being waiting patiently to be fed. A moment of deep, inner healing is too often lost in a hastily enumerated list of actions performed.

One evening an old Cherokee Indian spoke to his little grandson about a battle that goes on inside people. He said: "My son, the battle is between two wolves inside us all. One is evil. It is anger, envy, jealousy, sorrow, regret, greed, arrogance, self-pity, guilt, resentment, inferiority, lies, false pride, superiority, and ego. The other is good. It is joy, peace, love, hope, serenity, humility, kindness, benevolence, empathy, generosity, truth, compassion and faith."

The grandson thought about it for a minute and then asked: "Which wolf wins?"

The old Cherokee replied: "The one you feed."

Francis de Sales

ometimes the friends of God write of how they experienced hearing a phrase or a word which profoundly influenced their lives. This 'word' may not have been heard with their physical ears. It may have come as an intuition, heard by 'the ear of the heart', but with such clarity and force that it seemed to have been spoken aloud.

In the fourth century, a young orphan named Antony heard a preacher quoting the words of Jesus: "Go, sell what you have, give to the poor ... come follow me ... take no care for tomorrow..." [49] He understood those words as spoken directly to him. He sold his possessions, put his sister in the care of some pious women, and retired to a cave in the desert for 25 years. He was St Antony of the Desert, the greatest of those Desert Fathers.

In the thirteenth century, Francis of Assisi discovered a crucifix in an old abandoned chapel. As he prayed before the figure on the cross, he 'heard' it saying to him: "Francis, rebuild my Church." Francis later came to understand just what the words meant for him and for the whole of Christendom.

Early in 1537 Ignatius of Loyola and his companions journeyed to Rome in order to place themselves at the service of the Pope. At La Storta, a town on the outskirts of Rome, Ignatius had a vision in which he saw God the Father placing him next to his Son Jesus. Ignatius 'heard' the words of God: "I will be propitious to you in Rome."

These 'inner words' heard by the friends of God in the ear of the heart opened up a world of meaning which gave their lives purpose, direction, and energy.

Something like this happened in the late sixteenth century to a young Frenchman who was tempted to discouragement and even despair by the thought, strongly held by many at the time, that each person was predestined: either to heaven or to hell. The young man lived for some weeks in an agony of conscience, until one day, kneeling before a statue of Our Lady of Deliverance in the Paris church of St. Etienne-des-Grès, he 'heard' a voice distinctly saying: "I do not call myself the damning One: my name is Jesus." This single moment had a profound effect on young Francis de Sales and influenced all his teaching and his life from then on. Francis became a priest, a bishop, a recognised 'learned teacher' of the Church, and a saint.

Francis came from a wealthy and noble family. He was born in 1567, the eldest of 13 children. He went to school at Annecy, and then studied for seven years at the Jesuit college in Paris. When he was 21, he took a degree in law at the University of Padua, but on coming home, he announced his wish to become a priest. His father opposed the idea. Francis was the eldest boy, and furthermore, his father had his eye on someone for Francis, an arrangement which would mean a 'good marriage' and a convenient one for the family. Later, however, his father withdrew his opposition to Francis' decision, and Francis continued his studies for the priesthood and was ordained in 1593.

In 1594 Francis went to the Chablais region, where the impact of the Reformation had been very strong. Francis volunteered to undertake a mission of evangelisation of the area. Many people were converted as a result of his energy, his knowledge, and above all, his kindness. He was appointed assistant to the Bishop of Geneva, and three years later became bishop of that diocese. Together with St Jane Frances de Chantal, he founded the Institute of the Visitation of the Blessed Virgin, a religious congregation for women.

During his lifetime Francis preached more than 4,000 sermons and, in addition to his other activities, he was a spiritual director to a number of people. His advice was often given in the form of notes or letters, of which about 1,000 remain. Some of these were put together as the basis of the book for which Francis became famous: *The Introduction to the Devout Life*. The work, which is a masterpiece of psychology, practical morality and common sense, was immediately hailed as a classic, a reputation it has consistently maintained. It was translated into many different languages even in the lifetime of the author, and it has since gone through innumerable editions.

Francis' main concern was to assure people that holiness is compatible with a life 'in the world', contrary to the writings of other contemporary authors who regarded holiness as possible only by withdrawing from the world. Soldiers, husbands, housewives, people working in the town or country are all called by God to holiness. The practical ways of reaching holiness of life are simple: recalling the presence of God during one's day, having the right intention in whatever one does, and offering short prayers to God – like the "sharp darts of longing love" recommended in *The Cloud of Unknowing*. The main task of any Christian is to set his or her compass towards being faithful to God, to remember God during one's day and to do one's job with as much love as possible. It's as simple as that.

The doctrine of the book is set out with warmth, charm, gentleness, and in words that are clear and intelligible. This style no doubt accounts for much of its popularity up to the present day. But what accounts for the gentleness of his teaching was largely the experience he had in the church in Paris. Kneeling before the statue of Our Lady, venerated as Our Lady of Deliverance, the voice he heard was that of Jesus, who reminded Francis that mercy will always be found in the judgment of God. The influence of this experience stayed with Francis, and inspired a teaching that was radical for those Reformation times and for the subsequent times of Jansenism in the Catholic Church.

THE FALL IN THE DITCH

Well, my poor heart, here we are, fallen into the ditch which we had made so firm a resolution to avoid; Let us implore the mercy of God, and trust that He will help us to be more steadfast in the future, and let us place ourselves again on the path of humility. Courage! Henceforth let us be more on our guard: God will help us and we shall do well enough.

St Francis de Sales, Introduction to the Devout Life

ADMIT IT! FACE IT! THEN LEAVE IT!

In the course of our journey in the Spirit we are confronted by many paradoxes. One of the significant ones concerns the mystery of sin, grace, failure and redemption. On the one hand we discover that the Christian life involves a struggle from which we can't disengage ourselves. On the other hand we believe that the victory is already ours through Jesus Christ.

St Paul understood both sides of this paradox. Convinced that the Christian life is a struggle against super-powers, he writes to the people of Ephesus: "We are not fighting against human beings but against the wicked spiritual forces in the heavenly world: the rulers, authorities and cosmic powers of this dark age. So, put on God's armour now!" [50]

That's fighting talk! And yet when Paul concludes his reflections on his personal struggle with the forces warring within himself, his words contain both a cry of desperate need and a reply of confident victory: "Who will rescue me from this body of death? Thanks be to God, who does this through our Lord Jesus Christ!" [51]

We could put this another way. There is a sense in which we can truly say that, through Christ's death and resurrection, we have already been saved. As St Peter says: "We have a sure hope, and the promise of an inheritance that can never be spoiled or soiled, and can never fade away. It is being kept for you in the heavens." [52]

And so, in a way we need to do nothing but let it all happen. Whether through our contact with the Word of God in Scripture, in those special experiences called 'sacraments' in the formal sense or in the day-to-day 'sacramental' encounters with God, He wants to save us, and nothing can prevent this, unless we do.

And then there is the other side of the coin. We are called to an active engagement with the forces within us which limit our freedom to respond to God's love. Sooner or later we come to realise that the enemy is within. We become aware that the field of struggle between good and evil is not an arena outside of us, but in fact is within each one of us. As we mature, we realise that global evil is only a magnification of the civil war going on inside each individual, and we become aware that there is enough evidence in our personal lives to convince us that there is no crime we could not personally commit, given the right circumstances, though there may be some to which we are individually more inclined than others.

And so, one basic conviction found in all Christian writings since the New Testament is that the way of God is a daily cross. It is a journey which involves facing self-centredness and even evil outside of ourselves. But more dramatically, it involves facing that same spirit of self-centredness and that tendency to evil within ourselves. The friends of God understood clearly that the pilgrim is going to be beset by sin and failure. In our journey through life we are going to fall into the ditch.

But, what do we actually do about our failures? What is the Christian to believe about sin, and what is the Christian to do about its effects? And how does the Christian look at his or her frail humanity?

From the start, the Christian view of humanity has been, shall we say, realistically cautious. By that I mean that Christian faith has helped us to avoid the two extremes of excessive optimism about the possibilities for good we all have, and excessive pessimism which may lead us to think that our human nature is fundamentally corrupt, and that our bodies are simply a cage in which our soul resides in some way. This excessive pessimism implies that the sooner we put our humanity aside the better.

The realistically cautious approach which Christians take helps us to see our human nature as wounded but perfectible. Wounded because we are flawed creatures, and the experience of life reminds us of this almost daily. But perfectible because we are made in the image and likeness of God, and there is nothing we cannot master with the help of the One who gives us strength.[53] The mighty power of Christ which St Paul writes of enables us to transcend our tendency to selfishness and to live for Christ and others.

This two-sided view of human capacities has been well put by St John:

"If we say we have no sin in us, we are deceiving ourselves, and refusing to admit the truth. But if we acknowledge our sin, the God who is faithful will forgive us and purify us. Jesus is the sacrifice that takes away our sins."[54]

So we come back to that question: "What do we do about sin?" Francis de Sales, in the image of the traveller in the ditch, puts it clearly:

Admit it – *"Here we are fallen in the ditch"*
Face it – *"Let us implore the mercy of God"*
Trust God – *"Trust that God will help us"*
And then leave it – *"We shall do well enough"*

In this, Francis presents the best expression of Christian optimism. Such a view is grounded in realism, challenges us to self-transcendence, and brings us to a spirit of hope. Among all the interior attitudes that a spiritual pilgrim has to deal with, there are two which are most pernicious. These are: *deception*, living by illusion or untruth, and in this way denying the possibility that one could sin; and *despair*, believing that having fallen from grace, one might not actually be forgiven by God.

One of the common themes in the stories from the desert was the theme of the monk who sinned. The main purpose of the stories was to offer an answer to the question: What – really – is sin? What is the real failure in the spiritual journey? From the stories the monks related, it is clear that as far as they were concerned, the heart of failure was not lust, anger, greed, vanity or pride. Rather it was living in a state of self-deception, especially the deception that encouraged them to think they could go it alone, and then despairing of forgiveness when they slipped or fell.

The great antidote to self-deception and despair is the virtue of humility. The origin of this word – *humus* or earth – gives an insight into its meaning. The humble person is the one who is down to earth, feet on the ground, realistic, honest and truthful about self and God. Humility is the attitude that enables us to make hard-nosed and realistic judgments about both our human fallibility and the grace and power of Christ. And humility is learned, not by studying its meaning in books and not even by praying about it. It is learned in battle, and through struggle.

For most of us the struggle will seldom be with forces outside ourselves. The struggle will be an interior one, and will usually be the struggle to believe that God is right there in the middle of our failures. The real Christian is the repentant sinner who rises again after falling, and who repeatedly gets up after repeatedly falling.

There's something very liberating in this Christian attitude to sin. As Julian of Norwich put it: "Sin must be; but sin shall not be a shame to humans, but a glory... The mark of sin shall be turned to honour. And all shall be well and all manner of thing shall be well."

Graham Greene was a novelist who often reflected on the mystery of sin and redemption. When I was studying theology, Greene's books were kept in a locked cupboard in the library, accessible only to mature students, and then only to be read during holidays. I think in those years he was considered a somewhat dangerous 'Catholic writer'. His books often tread that difficult path between the mystery of personal failure and the saving grace of God. In the end it was the Christian view of sin and redemption that gave him a sense of personal liberation. In an interview he gave with a journalist Greene said: "the basic element I admire in Christianity is its sense of moral failure. That is its very foundation. For once you're conscious of personal failure you become a little less fallible." That's the true foundation of Christian humility.

In several of his novels he uses the Catholic experience of Confession as the arena for his dangerous reflections on who is a saint and who is a sinner, and the even more dangerous question of whether moral perfection is the same as holiness. His novel *Brighton Rock* has a particularly moving scene in which the heroine Rose goes to Confession to an old rather broken-down priest after her suicide pact with Pinky has left Pinky dead and her alive. The priest has a cold, he smells of eucalyptus, and he whistles through his breath as he says to her:

"There was a man, a Frenchman, you wouldn't know about him, my child, who had the same idea as you. He was a good man, a holy man, and he lived in sin all his life, because he couldn't bear the idea that any soul could suffer damnation... The man decided that if any soul was going to be damned, he would be damned too. He never took the sacraments, he never married his wife in the Church. I don't know, my child, but some people think he was – well, a saint. I think he died in what we are told is mortal sin – I'm not sure: it was in the war; perhaps..." He sighed, and whistled, bending his old head. He said: "You can't conceive, my child, nor can I or anyone, the... appalling... strangeness of the mercy of God... We must hope and pray, hope and pray. The Church does not demand that we believe any soul is cut off from mercy."

"The appalling strangeness of the mercy of God"... That's a very power-ful way of expressing a mystery that we'll never fathom. We can never call God 'just' or 'merciful' because those words describe our limited understanding of justice and mercy. God doesn't fit into these catego-ries. The mercy of God is beyond our comprehension. This is what we rely on when we fall into our ditches of sin and failure.

Some years ago I was called by a family to visit a family member who had been arrested for an offence which involved obsessive and compulsive behaviour. The man's arrest was a traumatic experience for his family who had no idea of the private life he had been leading for several years. As I made my way to the police station, I was at a loss as to what to do or say. I was not at all sure what I would find. I think I expected to see a man crushed by humiliation and shame. To my sur-prise I was confronted by a man whose face reflected a strange sense of peace and tranquillity. He explained to me: "For years I've carried this heavy weight, this private life, this secret sin. I couldn't find any way of telling anybody. I didn't believe that anyone would understand or accept me if I revealed this burden. But now at last it's all out in the open, and somehow I feel a tremendous burden lifted from me. I can now publicly face up to something that has been slowly and quietly devouring me for years."

I returned home wondering... Whatever one may think of the situation which brought this man and his family members to such a tragic and humiliating moment, one thing was evident. He had put himself on the path that St Francis de Sales recommends as we slip and slide through life:

"Admit it
Face it!
Trust God!
And then leave it!"

Gregory of Nyssa

he fourth century could be considered one of the most remarkable centuries in the history of Christian spirituality.

By then the Roman Empire, with its capital in Rome, was beginning to crumble at the edges and implode at its centre. Constantine moved the capital of the Empire to Constantinople in 330, and the Byzantine Empire began its remarkable thousand-year existence. This was the time of the movement to the desert and the beginning of the phenomenon of Christian monasticism. It was a century of intense theological discussion, controversy and debate. It saw the first two of the great Councils of the Church, the First Council of Nicea in 325 and the First Council of Constantinople in 381, when the major issues of Christian belief were settled in what we today recite as the Nicene Creed. This was the 'golden age' of theology. Some of the great Doctors of the Church lived during this century: St Jerome, St Ambrose and St Augustine in the West; St Athanasius, St John Chrysostom, St Cyril of Alexandria, St Ephrem and three great men known as the Cappadocian Fathers in the East.

The best way to describe the Cappadocian Fathers is to begin with a remarkable family living in Cappadocia, now central Turkey. It is a family which counts six canonised saints among the two parents and 10 children. Even though other members of the family became more famous in history, perhaps the most remarkable member was St Macrina, known as the Younger (to distinguish her from her equally saintly grandmother of the same name). Macrina wished to establish an environment in which her brothers could study and meditate, and where their mother Emmelia could find a place of peace. Macrina fostered the education of three of her brothers: Basil the second oldest of the brothers, Gregory, and Peter the youngest. All three brothers became bishops.

Two of the brothers, Basil and Gregory, were joined by a friend, Gregory of Nazianzen, and these three are recognised as the great Cappadocian Fathers. They set out to demonstrate that Christians need not fear any discussions with learned Greek-speaking intellectuals. The Cappadocian Fathers are credited with defining the Christian orthodox faith of the Eastern Roman Empire, as Augustine was to do in the West.

Basil, who became the bishop of Caesarea, was the most politically skilled churchman of the group. Gregory of Nazianzus was a brilliant orator, best known for his five 'theological orations', which succinctly summarised the thinking of the Cappadocian Fathers. But the deepest thinker of the three was Basil's brother Gregory, who became Bishop of Nyssa. In a sense, Gregory of Nyssa stands in the middle of a continuum, summing up many of the ideas of his great predecessors, such as the Greek philosopher Plato, the Jewish philosopher Philo of Alexandria (c. 20 BCE–c. 54 CE) and the Christian thinker Origen (c. 185–254 CE). He also initiated themes that would appear in the writings of the most prominent of the later Byzantine thinkers, notably Pseudo-Dionysius (c. 500) and Gregory Palamas (1296–1359). Through them, Gregory of Nyssa has also had an influence on modern European thought.

Born around 330, Gregory married and spent several years of his life in secular employment before he became a priest and then Bishop of Nyssa in 371. In the last years of his life, he travelled a great deal; he was in great demand as a preacher, teacher, and spiritual writer.

Gregory was an admirer of Origen's teachings, though he did not follow Origen in everything, in particular Origen's belief was that the human soul was not only immortal, but also eternal, and that it had existed previously in a pure state, enjoying a direct vision of God. According to Origen, the task of the human soul was to somehow to return to the state it had enjoyed before becoming part a human body. Gregory doesn't follow this theory of pre-existent souls. There is no connection between the Creator and the created. God dwells in the deepest darkness, a point which Gregory stresses in his writings on mystical theology.

Gregory is most known for his commentaries on the Song of Songs and on the Beatitudes, as well as his treatises on the Trinity. He is probably best known for two significant works of mystical theology, *From Glory to Glory* and *The Life of Moses*.

In *The Life of Moses*, Gregory follows a line carved out by the Desert Fathers and Mothers and by Origen, who described the spiritual journey as a journey taking place in three stages. Springing from the Book of Exodus, Gregory reflects that having been delivered from slavery to selfishness we are led to Mount Sinai to meet God at the summit. But whereas Origen had described the spiritual journey as a passage from darkness to light, Gregory reverses the image, and describes the journey as passing from light to darkness. He uses the three experiences of Moses as symbols of this journey:

a) the revelation of the burning bush (*phos* – light)
b) the ascent of Moses into the mist of the mountain (*nephele* – obscurity)
c) the entry of Moses into the darkness of the cloud (*gnophos* – darkness).

The reason for this reversal is simple. Origen saw the soul as returning from the darkness of its fallen state to the light of its original state. For Gregory the movement is to come from the light of revelation to the experience of God who is utterly unknowable. Paradoxically, it is only through not-knowing and not-seeing that God can be known and seen. Gregory is one of the great representatives of the 'mysticism of darkness', or *apophatic* theology.

Gregory of Nyssa died around the year 395 and is revered as one of the greatest of the Eastern Church Fathers. His discovery by the West brought about one of the most active periods of spiritual writing in the twelfth century.

THE CHEERING SPECTATORS

*At horse races the spectators, intent on victory, shout to their
favourites in the contest, even though the horses are eager to
run. From the stands they participate in the race with their eyes,
thinking to incite their charioteer to keener effort, at the same
time urging the horses on while leaning forward and flailing the
air with their outstretched hands instead of a whip.*

*They do this not because their actions themselves contribute
anything to the victory; but in this way, by their good will, they
eagerly show in voice and deed their concern for the contestants.*

*I seem to be doing the same thing myself, most valued friend and
brother. While you are competing admirably in the divine race
along the course of virtue, light-footedly leaping and straining
constantly for the prize of the heavenly calling, I exhort, urge,
and encourage you vigorously to increase your speed.*

Gregory of Nyssa, The Life of Moses

"Give me a word by which I may be saved!"

The striking image of the cheering crowd at a stadium is consistent with Gregory of Nyssa's understanding of our Christian journey. In the depth of our hearts, Gregory says, there is a "longing", a "desire" for something beyond us, for a true home that we haven't yet discovered, for someone to whom we belong with heart and soul. This longing makes us restless, mobile, searching and stretching towards something beyond. It makes us go "light-footedly leaping and straining" on the journey. Gregory uses the word *epektasis* to describe this movement of stretching out, pushing forward.

This is the work of each Christian; no one else can do it for us. In his image, Gregory reminds us that the race belongs to the horses and their riders. The horses are eager to run, the riders are urging them on. But only they are on the field. The spectators can't affect the outcome. They "participate in the race with their eyes"; but their voices and gestures "contribute nothing to the victory" which belongs to the horses or the athletes. In the spiritual contest, says Gregory, the participant is alone in the race.

But not quite alone. In Gregory's image, the spectators do play an important part. They are concerned for the contestants. They urge the horses on from a distance, "leaning forward and flailing the air with their outstretched hands instead of a whip". These signs of encouragement don't directly contribute to the victory, but imagine if the crowd was silent! So, says Gregory, a person on the spiritual journey needs the encouragement of others.

Then comes a beautiful thought from Gregory, almost hidden in a parenthesis. Gregory addresses his reader as a "most valued friend and brother". He sees his reader as a true companion, and a most valued one at that. He doesn't see himself as a teacher or instructor. He is not a potter turning a lump of clay into some image which he has in mind. He is not an artist making his work a reflection of his or her perceptions, insights or emotions. Nor is he like a traffic controller putting law and order into the chaotic movement of the traffic of another's life. If Gregory has anything to offer, it is his encouragement and the testimony that he himself is on the journey with this most valued friend and brother.

Most of us are familiar with what we call "spiritual direction", which is what Gregory is talking about. Our current understanding of the Western tradition of spiritual direction may be enriched when we look at three other approaches to spiritual accompaniment. These approaches come from the Desert tradition, from the Russian tradition and from the Celtic tradition.

The Abba and Amma of the Desert Tradition

A Christian went into the desert with one big question in mind: "How can I be saved?" The monk's first task was to find an *abba* (spiritual father) or an *amma* (spiritual mother) who could help the monk to initiate or continue the spiritual journey. The *abba* or *amma* was one who had already discovered some of the landmarks and the pitfalls that one finds on the journey, and who was competent in distinguishing the authentic from the apparent. The collected *Sayings of the Desert Fathers* show that the request most frequently put to the *abba* or *amma* was: "Give me a word by which I may be saved."

The *abba's* reply – if it came – was short, usually laconic and always directed to a particular individual with a particular need. It was a word which created a dialogue between the monk and the monk's inner self. The word was not to be discussed, analysed or disputed in any way. At times, it was not even fully understood. But it was to be memorised and absorbed into life.

An *abba* was not to be consulted over trivial details of one's life, but over the major questions of how to live fully. Visits to one's *abba* were not frequent. There is the story of *abba* Macarius and the two young strangers who came to him for guidance. He showed them where to live and left them alone for three years before he inquired any further about them.

Sometimes the monk himself didn't think it necessary even to ask a question of the *abba*. Three brothers were in the habit of visiting the great St Antony every year. The first two asked him questions about salvation. The third said nothing. Eventually, Antony said to him, "You have been coming here to see me for a long time now and you never ask me any questions." The other replied, "One thing is enough for me, Father; to see your face." [55]

The *abba* had one great duty in regard to the disciple, and that was the duty of intercessory prayer. Quite often the intensity of the *abba's* or *amma's* intercession was so great that they were led to weep for their disciple. Weeping for oneself and for others became a common practice in the desert. This probably explains the extraordinary compassion that holy *abbas* had for their disciples, and conversely the great love that disciples had for their *abbas*, so much so that even the death of the *abba* did not require that a disciple should look for a replacement.

When we read the stories coming out of the Desert tradition, we are not surprised to read the sorts of titles that the tradition gave to the spiritual guide: doctor, counsellor, intercessor, mediator. We may be surprised, though, at one descriptive title: the *abba* was to be a sponsor (*anadochus*) on behalf of his spiritual child. An *anadochus* was one who took responsibility for another's inner state of soul, like someone going on bail for another. The word was applied particularly to Jesus who took on the sins of mankind. An *abba* who took on the role of sponsor for his spiritual child didn't merely pray for his child, but took on his shoulders the weight of their temptations and guilt.

This role of sponsor is a dangerous role, and one which any spiritual guide would not take on lightly. In the sixth century, Barsanuphius, the famous Desert Father from Gaza, wrote to his spiritual disciples: "I care for you more than you care for yourself... I am bearing your burdens and your offences... You are like someone sitting under a shady tree... I would gladly lay down my life for you." [56]

Barsanuphius took upon himself the sins of Dorotheus of Gaza, who was tormented by his sexual life that he had not brought fully under control. That was truly the role of a sponsor.

But the role was not to be a one-sided affair. The disciple had to be actively involved. Once a brother came to St Antony and said: "Pray for me." Antony replied: "I will have no mercy upon you, nor will God have any, if you yourself do not make an effort and if you do not pray to God." [57] Barsanuphius took on the role of *anadochus* for Dorotheus, but Dorotheus in return promised never to forget the mercy of God, and to keep himself from pride and gossip.

What was important was the relationship between the monk and the *abba*, whose vocation it was, as Gregory's image implies, "to exhort, urge, and encourage" his disciple, and to watch with compassion as he went "light-footedly leaping" on the journey.

The Staretz in the Russian tradition

Russia became Christian in 988, and monastic life took root quickly. Russian Christianity was shaped by the Byzantine Empire of the East. The Desert title of *abba* came to be translated as *staretz* in Russia. The word literally means an elder, but a *staretz* does not have to be old. He could be relatively young, but mature in the spiritual gifts of wisdom, understanding and insight. In the Russian Church the role of the *staretz* was similar to that of the *abba* of the Desert tradition but with some nuances.

A person taking initial steps on the path to God was first advised: "Find the Map!" The "Map" was the tradition of spirituality already accumulated and written down from the time of the Desert Fathers and the lived experience of other elders. A *staretz* was very careful to shape his advice according to The Map left by his ancestors.

A striking feature of the lives of the Russian *startsy* was their deeply ascetical preparation. Most of them spent long years in total isolation in the forests of Russia before finally emerging to help others. These personal ascetical struggles left the *staretz* with the gift of discernment which enabled him to 'read the inner life' of another, and to provide spiritual guidance exactly tempered to the needs of a particular individual at a particular time. Some *startsy* were said to know the thoughts and secrets of those who came to them before they had said a word, and many *startsy* were also thought to have powers of healing, clairvoyance, and prophecy.

The *staretz* took little interest in the detailed confession of their penitents. His interest was the movements of the heart, and the orientation of the whole of a person's life.

Consulting a *staretz* has always been considered a normal practice in the Russian Church. Dostoevesky gives a good description of the Russian *staretz* in his novels, particularly in *The Brothers Karamazov*.

The Anam Cara in the Celtic Tradition

The Celtic world lay outside the limits of the Roman Empire, and

Celtic spirituality has a different 'feel' from the Christian spirituality that developed within the administrative and cultural environment of the Roman Empire.

The wisdom of the peoples who eventually settled in Ireland, Scotland, Wales, Cornwall, the Isle of Man, Brittany and Galicia has had an influence on the way Celtic spirituality has developed and the forms it has taken.

In Celtic spirituality, there is a beautiful understanding of love and friendship. Celtic culture recognises that although the human body is born complete in one moment, the human heart is never completely born. So 'life in the heart' is always something to be cultivated. Out of this, in the religious context, came the need for the *anam cara* or 'soul-friend'. *Anam* is the Gaelic word for soul, and cara is the word for friend. In the early Celtic Church, the *anam cara* was a person who acted as a companion; not necessarily an expert in the science of the soul, but proficient in the friendship of the soul. This person was originally someone to whom one confessed, revealing the hidden intimacies of one's life, sharing one's innermost self, mind and heart.

An old Celtic proverb notes that a "person without a soul-friend is like a body without a head". The notion of the 'soul-friend' suggests a somewhat unstructured and informal relationship, unlike our present understanding of spiritual direction.

In each of these three traditions the gift of spiritual accompaniment was not restricted to clergy. Spiritual friendship, accompaniment, discernment and companionship are gifts from God and are given to people regardless of gender or vocation.

Most of us hope that when the moment comes for us to cross the great divide between life and death there will be someone with us at least to encourage us in that last moment. But even while we live there's a great divide that faces us, and that is the divide between our false self and our real self; between the face we turn outward to others and the face we turn inwards to ourselves; between our inner self and our outer self. This is a gap that's as wide as the gap between death and life. How blessed we are if we have found someone who is able to encourage us in our journey through life! And what a blessing it would be for someone else if we took up the ministry of intercession – even to the point of weeping tears – for them on their journey!

Hesychius of Sinai

here is a lot of confusion about the identity of a writer named Hesychius. In the early centuries of the Christian era there were at least six significant people who had the same name, and often they and their works are confused. For a long time the man of which this chapter speaks was confused with another Hesychius, known as Hesychius of Jerusalem, who was a Biblical scholar of the fifth century. Hesychius of Sinai on the other hand seems to have been a priest and a monk living on Mt Sinai in the monastery of the Thorn Bush, of which he was the superior. He is familiar with and quotes from *The Ladder of Divine Ascent* of St John Climacus, which dates him to about the seventh or eighth century.

Even though we don't know very much about the man, his name tells us a lot. The name Hesychius comes from the Greek *hesychia* which means tranquility, peace and calm, and this name has been given to a style of spirituality that developed in the area of Sinai around the time of this author's life. Hesychius makes frequent reference to this style of spirituality both explicitly and implicitly.

The word *hesychia* and its derivatives took on several shades of meaning. At a most basic level, a *hesychast* was simply a monk who lived alone, apart from others. At another level a monk seeking *hesychia* was a monk who not only lived apart from others, but who even, in his isolated cell, lived a life truly alone and without distraction. Later, the title *hesychast* was given to a monk who had emptied his heart of passions and who practiced uninterrupted prayer. His prayer was prayer which put aside all thoughts, which halted any activity of the intellect, and which remained pure, naked and empty before God.

From this practice of *hesychia* a form of spirituality developed. This spirituality stresses the importance of interior and exterior calmness and vigilance, of attentiveness and watchfulness over one's thoughts so as to leave the heart free for prayer. This stillness and calmness is not only silence or the absence of noise, but an attitude of listening to God and of openness to God. It is not a passive state of mind, but an active vigilance, a careful watching, an attentive listening.

This state of tranquillity and peace is the seed-bed for what came to be known as hesychastic prayer. When the mind, free of thoughts, descends into the heart, the heart then becomes the place where deep contemplative prayer takes place. We associate the practice of hesychastic prayer particularly with Sinai in the seventh and eighth centuries, and with Mt Athos in subsequent centuries and up to the present day. Hesychasm is a significant element in Russian spirituality. It is the spirituality presented in the *Philokalia*.

The tradition of hesychastic prayer was characterised by three stages. The first stage was the practice of asceticism and self-discipline. The aim of this stage was to become free from the disorders of mind and heart that impede a life of prayer. A second stage was to prepare the heart of the disciple for contemplative prayer. Sometimes physical techniques such as breathing or proper posture were also used to help to bring about an external stillness of body, and this would in turn help to create the internal *hesychia* of heart in which silent prayer might grow. The Christian might then arrive at a third stage of direct and personal intimate knowledge of God.

Out of this Hesychastic spirituality, also called "the spirituality of the heart", grew what we know today as the "Jesus Prayer", a way of praying very common to the East, and recently rediscovered and practised in the West. The Jesus Prayer consists of a simple and constant repetition of a phrase from the Gospel: "Lord Jesus Christ, Son of God, have mercy on me, a sinner." This was the cry of Bartimaeus who sat on the side of the road as Jesus walked past and who begged to be cured of his blindness.[58] In a dozen words, Bartimaeus summed up the deepest desire of his heart. Jesus cured him of his blindness, and the tradition of the early Church saw in that one sentence a sort of summary of essential elements of Christian belief: Jesus is Lord, Jesus is Son of God, Jesus brings us the salvation that we need.

The inclusion of these ideas in the Church has recommended this as a very effective way of praying. The prayer is simply repeated over and over, slowly and peacefully, while savouring the meaning of each of the words. The prayer is first of all recited quietly with the lips, then it is held in the mind, and finally it descends into the heart and eventually remains there, even while the person may be occupied with other things. Many writers recommend that the prayer could be recited to the rhythm of one's breathing: saying the first part of the prayer as one breathes in, the second part as one breathes out, the third as one breathes in and the last phrase as one breathes out.

Hesychius wrote a treatise entitled *On Watchfulness and Holiness* which is one of the most important texts in the *Philokalia*. The work deals with the themes of inner peace, watchfulness and tranquility, and in it Hesychius makes explicit and frequent reference to the Jesus Prayer. Quite simply, he stresses that the recital of the Jesus Prayer or even simply the invocation of the name of Jesus has a powerful influence on any 'inner work' that a Christian faces, especially the work of watchfulness or *nepsis*. The single-phrased Jesus Prayer destroys the work of the forces of darkness within a person,[59] and through this prayer the mind is cleared of the dark clouds that cross it.[60] "Trying to do this inner work without using the Jesus Prayer, Hesychius says, "is like trying to cross the ocean without a boat." [61]

The image of the dancing dolphins comes from his treatise *On Watchfulness and Holiness*.

THE DANCING DOLPHINS

After having purified and unified our minds by the Jesus Prayer,
our thoughts swim like happy dolphins in a calmed sea.

Hesychius of Sinai, On Watchfulness and Holiness

"In the stillness is the dancing"

An elderly and rather holy priest once said to me, "You know, when I was a child I used to pray quite well and quite often, I think. Then when I began my studies in theology, everything became very complicated. And I've spent all these years trying to pray as I used to when I was a child."

The comment is not so atypical. I think there are many people who might say something similar. I've often asked myself: "Why do we make something which is so basic to us as humans so complicated?" Things that seem to come naturally to us as children, like playing, using our imagination, being spontaneous or expressing ourselves simply and directly, all seem to move off our screen as we become adults.

Towards the end of his life, Pablo Picasso wrote, "I've spent all my life learning to draw like a child." A walk through the Picasso Museum in Barcelona, Spain, gives a viewer a wonderful insight into what this meant for Picasso. His early paintings, in particular his *First Communion* painted in 1895 when he was only 14, show what a prodigy Picasso was, and how even at an early age he could master the rules of the classical style of painting. Then, as he broke from the classic style, he went through many different periods in his style of art: the blue period, the rose period, the Paris period, the African period, the cubist period. To those who expect art to reflect some literal reality, Picasso's later paintings become more and more difficult to understand. These people find the last rooms dedicated to Picasso's cubist paintings somewhat confusing and overpowering. It's fascinating to see that in these same rooms children move freely and with great interest, fascinated by the colours, shapes and forms which so clearly excite them and strike their capacity to imagine. Something in Picasso's later style releases the spontaneity and creativity in young viewers.

So why does something like prayer, which many of us may have done easily as children, now become complicated – or perhaps even a dead issue in our lives as adults?

Life changes us, of course, and it is to be expected that what came easily to us as children no longer does so as adults. Our physical and emotional centre of gravity changes and we need to develop new skills to keep physically and psychologically balanced. Life deals out its difficult cards, and we have to develop ways to stop ourselves from falling into cynicism or sadness. We slip into hardened attitudes and prejudices, and we need to find ways of keeping alive the child's sense of wonder and curiosity. Of course, as we get older we need to put away the things of the child. But it is a shame that as some of us put away the toys of the child, we also put away things that would serve us well in adulthood – things like wonder, openness, curiosity and the ability to celebrate.

This is why Hesychius' image of the dancing dolphins has something to say to us. It's rather surprising to find this image used by someone who lived in the middle of the Sinai Desert. But for me, coming from an island nation surrounded by sea, the image is very evocative.

There are not many scenes that so quickly send my mind back to the carefree days of summer, of holidays, of play, of fun, of rest, as this image of dolphins frolicking in the calm sea. There was a year in my childhood when our nation became quite famous for its tame and friendly dolphin, Opo, who passed the whole summer in a small bay, playing alongside children, letting them ride on her back, accompanying the children's laughter with her shrill calls. The freedom of the children, the friendliness of Opo, the sunny time of holiday, simply highlighted the fact that the best environment for those who play is tranquility. Children play best when they are untroubled, when they are not in competition with each other, when they don't have to prove anything to themselves or to others. I suspect those are the very qualities we lose as we become adults.

This is why Hesychius' image catches our attention. Tranquility is the best environment for those who play. Hesychius suggests that it is also the best environment for those who pray. In fact, he belongs to the tradition that tells us that tranquility is the *essential* environment for prayer. When the body, the mind and the spirit are at peace, then the spring of prayer can be released.

Through his image, Hesychius seems to propose three handy rules for praying. First, immerse yourself in the presence of God.

The dolphins play freely and happily because they are surrounded, nourished and supported by the sea. We might begin our prayer by imagining God as a sea surrounding us, supporting us, giving us life, and enabling us to move freely and peacefully.

Second, establish yourself in stillness. This is a little more difficult. Hesychius' tradition speaks of three freedoms essential for this state of stillness or tranquility: freedom from anger, freedom from fear and freedom from obsessive thoughts.

The trouble with anger, says Hesychius' tradition, is that very often it hides itself from our consciousness, or it masquerades as something else. Many are surprised when they realise that some of their physical ailments are actually the body's reaction to anger. Some are shocked to realise that what they thought was a deep sadness in them is rage that has been told to keep quiet. Often enough, depression is nothing other than quelled anger.

Anger often goes hand in hand with fear; each of them impedes our tranquility. Many people suffer from crippling fears – fear for their future, fear of their past, fear of the unknown, fear of what others may think, fear of failure, fear of being found out – and so the list goes on.

These fears often express themselves in troublesome or obsessive thoughts. We catch ourselves recalling the same story of a hurt inflicted on us; we find ourselves making speeches in our minds; we catch ourselves thinking how we might pay back someone who has hurt us. These obsessive and recurring thoughts take away our inner freedom and prevent genuine prayer from happening. Hesychius says that inner peace is a state of silence "unbroken by thoughts".

As we've seen, from the earliest centuries, anyone who seriously took up the inner journey soon discovered that one of the greatest obstacles in the path was troublesome thoughts, or *logismoi*. Wise teachers of the way of prayer proposed two ways of dealing with these thoughts. One of these was the technique of "talking back" to the thoughts (*antirrhesis*), using some appropriate words from the Scriptures to refute the troublesome thought. The difficulty with that method is that it required a good deal of memorisation of Scripture, a skill which many of us don't have.

Hesychius provides us with a simpler approach, and this is the basis of his third, useful rule for prayer: recite the Jesus prayer. From apostolic times the name of Jesus has always been regarded as powerful and able to work wonders. In his words to his followers, Jesus promised them that whatever they asked for in his name they would be given, and that whatever they did in his name would carry his power.[62] The disciples took this seriously and literally. *The Acts of the Apostles* contain many instances of what happened when people called on or acted in the name of Jesus. Peter and John cured a lame man by ordering him to walk "in the name of Jesus Christ the Nazarene." [63]

Over the centuries many people of all different walks of life have tried this way of praying and have found that it works. I'm one of those people. My life has been a full life of teaching and administration. The years of teaching required concentration, preparation, study – all mind-filling things. It was not easy to sit down and pray with one's mind full of thoughts buzzing round. The years of administration involved large amounts of travel. Crossing date-lines and passing through time zones often left me wondering what time – or even what day – it was. I've had to spend hours waiting in airports or train stations. I've often not had the luxury of a structured day in which prayer can be a defined and well-prepared moment. Like many people, I often dreamed of that mythic opportunity which monks who live in a monastery seem to have – a regular and rhythmical day where everything leads to the experience of prayer. I know it was, is and will be a myth.

During all those years, the Jesus Prayer has been my customary way of praying. When I've had to snatch a brief moment for prayer on the run, or when I've found myself stranded in an airport waiting for the screen to tell me that my plane is finally ready for boarding, using the Jesus Prayer has been a wonderful way of easing tension or calming annoyance.

When I've found the space for some more tranquil time for prayer, the Jesus Prayer somehow has kept my mind from dozing off and chasing after any of the countless thoughts that race around in my head.

There have been the times, too, when the prayer has stayed with me, repeating itself inside me as I went about other activities. This is what many others have experienced when they use the prayer.

But the masters of the spiritual life issue a word of warning: Be careful! This prayer, though it is simple, is also dangerous. Calling on the name of Jesus makes Jesus present in a very real way. And the Jesus who comes when called through the Jesus Prayer is the same Jesus who walked on earth; and he will do the same things to us now as he did then to others. This is the Jesus "who went about doing good", [64] and who brought joy to others; [65] but he is also the one who can recognise, name and cast out demons, [66] who "speaks with authority" to the forces of evil, [67] who can face me with everything I have ever done, [68] who confronts me with the truth about myself,[69] who enters into my places of death and darkness and brings life and light.[70] This is the Jesus who made people grateful for his miracles; but who also made them afraid of his power, even to the point of asking him to back off and leave them alone. [71] All the things that Jesus did to others during his life on earth he will do with me and in me.

This is one reason why people are advised to find a spiritual guide or director if they begin seriously to pray the Jesus Prayer. Fear and self-deception are always near at hand.

Jesus' words are our source of hope. He promises us: "I have come so that you will have life, and more life, and more life."[72] And after that: "Do not be afraid." Hesychius also gives us confidence. He connects the recitation of the Jesus Prayer with inner peace. The prayer comes as a result of inner peace and it also creates inner peace. When the heart is at peace, it can pray the prayer spontaneously; and on the other hand, when the heart is not at peace, the name of Jesus often and rhythmically repeated will bring it peace.

In this image of the dancing dolphins, Hesychius paints a very attractive and liberating picture of the way of prayer. He stresses the sense of peace and joy that it brings to the heart, and the fruitfulness that comes from it. "The more the rain falls on the earth, the softer it makes it; similarly, the more we call upon Christ's Holy Name, the greater the rejoicing and exultation that it brings to the earth of our heart." [73]

Jean-Joseph Surin

 n the 1630s, Loudun, a town of the Province of Poitou in France, became the setting for strange happenings. A community of Ursuline nuns fell victim to apparent diabolical possession. For two years the community was in chaos. A parish priest of the area, Urbain Grandier, was accused of bringing the devil into the convent. Grandier was tried, found guilty of witchcraft, and then burnt at the stake. Meanwhile the community of nuns, especially the Prioress, Jeanne des Anges, continued to display symptoms of diabolical possession. Many attempts were made to rid the nuns of this affliction, but with no success. Eventually, the bishop asked a Jesuit priest, renowned for his outstanding goodness and knowledge of the spiritual life, to take on the difficult mission of exorcising the convent.

At first this priest, Jean-Joseph Surin, was no more successful than his predecessors had been. More than that, he himself fell victim to this strange phenomenon. In his desire to save the Prioress, he offered to accept the evil spirit that was possessing her, if this would ultimately free her. It seems his offer was accepted. "During my ministry, the devil passed from the body of the possessed person and entered into mine," he wrote to a friend.[74] Jeanne des Anges was liberated. But from that moment, Surin's time of interior and exterior trial began.

For the next 20 years he seemed to be possessed, undergoing awful trials and suffering. He found no consolation in things of the Spirit; he became convinced that he was damned. Twice he was tempted to commit suicide by throwing himself out a window. In his autobiography he writes that he lost the power to communicate, becoming unable to speak for seven months. He was unable to celebrate the Eucharist, or to read or to write. He suffered from acute sensitivity of the nerves, and was not able to dress or undress himself, or make any kind of movement without great physical pain. His doctors could find no explanation for his sickness, and nor could they find any cure.[75]

Curiously, according to one of his biographers, during this time of obsession he retained a remarkable ability to preach.

"It is true he was unable to prepare himself for this by any reading or study, but on entering the pulpit and making the sign of the cross a wonderful transformation was manifest. His vigourous mind instantly gained the ascedancy; his powerful voice and facile oratory won universal attention and admiration. His physician declared it miraculous." [76]

In the evening of Surin's life, the sky cleared. In 1658, his troubles ended and were followed by a time of great consolation. He developed a vast ministry of spiritual direction, and he began to dictate his experiences and then to write books on the spiritual life. These books for many years became classic works of spiritual experience.

As a Jesuit, Surin was a follower of Ignatius of Loyola. Much of his spiritual writing concerns the discernment of spirits, good and evil. He was also a follower of Louis Lallemant, one of the great masters of French spirituality, and in turn he had a great influence on two great spiritual writers of the eighteenth century, Jean-Pierre de Caussade, and Jean Nicolas Grou.

Was Surin mad? Was he truly possessed? Or was he a victim soul? There are many different opinions on the matter, and from this distance of time it's not easy to make a balanced judgment. On the one hand, the great preacher Bossuet described him as "consumed with spirituality". By contrast, a contemporary Jesuit who knew him for 20 years said that "he led so deranged and shameful a life that one hardly dares speak of it. In the end it reached the point where the most wise attributed it all, quite correctly, I believe, to madness ... (Later) he wrote books and letters, visited his neighbour and spoke very well about God, but he never said his prayers, or read his Breviary, said Mass rarely and to his dying day mumped about and gesticulated in a ridiculous and absurd fashion". [77] A modern psychiatrist might describe his state as a state of classic catatonic schizophrenia. But perhaps Russian Christians would recognise and respect in him the characteristics of a "fool for Christ".

It's probably not important to make an assessment of these aspects of Surin's life. But what is important is this: Surin's life is dramatic evidence that God's power at work in us is not confined to or limited by our human categories of good/bad, sane/mad, perfect/imperfect or even morally good/bad. God acts in the cracks of human life. Surin believed that he gained insights into God not through an awareness of God's presence, but through the experience of God's absence. His life is a testimony that in the spiritual journey, the only way *out of* the desert is *through* it.

In the end, the acid test, probably, is the body of spiritual writing that Surin left behind. One cannot write lasting works on spirituality unless one has experienced for oneself the touch of God. Only a soul at peace could write of these things with lucidity. At least at the end of his life, his soul experienced that peace, and from that centre point came a source of power.

The extraordinary story of Jean-Joseph Surin and the events that shaped his life were popularised by Aldous Huxley in his book, *The Devils of Loudun* (1952). Ken Russell based his film *The Devils* on the story, and the film caused a sensation when it was released in 1973. The events of Loudun were also made into an opera which was produced in 1969.

It's not surprising that Surin found a musical image as the best way to describe what he wanted to say about the spiritual journey. Music is a good indicator of the state of the soul. Music creates healing and it reflects a healed spirit. Surin found that inner peace and unity of heart.

THE LUTE PLAYER

Just as the lute player keeps his instrument in harmony although
he hums a number of different tunes, provided the main chord
which sustains the ground-base for the song remains in the same
key, so, provided union of heart is maintained, one can strike
all the chords in one's prayer if they accord with this chief and
fundamental key.

Jean Joseph Surin, *Spiritual writings*

"Living from the inside out"

Surin's image of the lute player is well-chosen. In earlier times the lute was probably the most important instrument in use for secular music. Sometimes it was used as a solo instrument but more generally it was used to accompany a singer. The lute established the key and the basic rhythm to the song. Once this was set and the unity of the piece was established, the solo singer was free to improvise or extemporise. The occasional dissonance and disharmony did not detract from the good music that resulted; it even added colour and texture to it.

Surin knew what he was talking about when he used this image. To others, his external life must have seemed a life marked by dissonance and disharmony, but the inner core of his heart was set on God, and that created the unity and authenticity of his life. It was from this inner core that he acted.

Most of us begin to learn our behaviours by conforming our actions to external rules or expectations. This is a normal part of upbringing. From our earliest years we hear phrases like: "A good boy/girl does this", or "We don't do that in our family", or "These are the values of this school", or "Christian belief requires us to do this or that", or "Our company's mission is...."

This is all totally appropriate as a way of beginning to assimilate values for living. The trouble with learning this way, however, is that we risk learning to act "from the outside in". We learn what is required of us in our external conduct and we conform our actions to that measure. But there is no guarantee that this way of behaving will become a part of our personal belief system. And if our ways of behaving do not come from an inner conviction, then in times of stress or pressure, the fabric of our external conduct breaks down.

It is true that rules of politeness and etiquette demand that we act or talk in certain ways at certain times. Sometimes our role or function or profession may require us to dress or act in certain ways. But there is always a risk that we might identify with the role or the function or the way of dressing that accompany the task we do, and submerge our real identity under this *persona*. When this external mask collapses, all is revealed. Then Einstein's observation of the physical world becomes shockingly true for our personal lives: the last thing to collapse is the surface.

We've all met people who act from the outside in. Titles, appearance, reputation have an inflated importance for them. Saving face or keeping up appearances becomes a major preoccupation. Real relationships aren't possible with these people because there is no 'real' person to relate to. Carl Jung put it well when he wrote: "The brighter the *persona*, the darker the shadow." We're all instinctively suspicious of the person who is too good to be true. We know there is a flaw that has been carefully papered over. We are not surprised when the false *persona* crumbles. We are saddened but often not surprised when we learn that someone who was regarded as a pillar of society or of the Church is exposed as living another life in some deviant way.

There comes a time in our lives when we need to change our way of doing things and act from the inside out. People who live from the inside out have an unchallengeable authority in their lives. Their actions do not flow from an attempt to conform to an external norm or expectation, but instead come instinctively from within.

Vincent Van Gogh's paintings don't reproduce or replicate the reality he saw. They reflect how that reality hit his soul, which burned with the desire, as he wrote, "to bring comfort to people". This is precisely the effect that his paintings have on people – they express passion and evoke compassion in the viewer. Sergei Rachmaninov's music comes from an inner depth that is instantly recognisable. When Leonard Bernstein conducted an orchestra, he was not reproducing in sound what was written on a musical score. The music passed through his inner being to the audience.

One of the great memories of my early life was attending a concert in which the great cellist Jacqueline du Pre played. I don't remember whether she played the Dvorak Cello concerto or the Elgar concerto. What I do remember, and what is indelibly imprinted in my mind, is the sight of this woman playing; her cello almost a part of her, her long hair flying about as she played. One had the distinct impression that she was not playing the music; rather, the score, the cello, the whole experience was playing her. She was playing from the inside out.

When people live from the inside out, their external conduct, their words spoken or written, the music they played or conducted, the art they produced, have a power that cannot be stopped, and express a truth that cannot be contradicted.

Jesus acted 'from the inside out'. People noted the contrast between his conduct and the conduct of the Pharisees. When the Pharisees spoke, their words sounded hollow, and went nowhere. When Jesus spoke, his words came from somewhere inside his deepest self, and the people noted that "he spoke with authority".

What was the 'inside' from which Jesus acted? We get a hint of it from his experience in the desert. The Gospel writers tell us that he faced temptations at the end of his experience, and he triumphed over them by the famous three 'Noes': to greed, to pride, and to power. What's more important, though, is not what happened at the *end* of the experience, but what happened during that time, and *before* his temptations. It is here that we find the core or the 'inside' of Jesus, namely, what he said 'Yes' to. Like his Noes, his Yeses were three-fold: Yes to the Word of the Father, Yes to the Providence of the Father and Yes to worship of the Father. Whatever happened to Jesus in the desert, it was an experience in which he established the inner core of his being, or, to use Surin's image, where he established the key and the basenotes for the music of his life.

This 'inside' – where does it come from? Not necessarily from genius. There are many geniuses who do not act from the inside out, and many humble ordinary people who do. We'll probably never know what is the 'inside' or the bedrock out of which these people act. But in one of his songs, *Anthem*, Leonard Cohen gives us a clue:

> *"There is a crack, a crack in everything*
> *That's how the light gets in."*

Scratch the surface of the lives of these authentic people and you will probably find a 'crack in the heart', a fatal flaw perhaps, like a struggle with dark depression, compulsive behaviour or sexual fragility. Or there might have been some tragedy in their lives – loss of love, political exclusion, imprisonment for ideas – which has left its mark on their heart.

When the cracks in the heart first become apparent, at least to ourselves, we might react in different ways. We may try to paper over the cracks and pretend that they are not there. We create a false *persona*. But sooner or later those who paint or paper over the cracks find that the paint begins to peel off. However much we may want to deny them, nothing can hide the flaws in our cracked humanity. We forget that what we deny in ourselves is often all too obvious to others.

In the first decade of this century the Catholic Church faced scandals that it had never had to face before. The fabric of what people identified as the institutional church was exposed as corrosive and flawed. At the very moment when such things were being revealed, it was noticeable that greater attention was being paid to external aspects of Church life such as dress, language and ceremony. An attempt was made to create a more 'mystical' element in religious worship; vestments worn at religious ceremonies were more elaborately decorated; the mitres that bishops wore became bigger; some cardinals took to wearing the *cappa magna* – a long train of scarlet formerly used in ceremonies and processions. Was this a good way to respond to the flaws in the internal life of the Church? Painting over cracks is never a healthy response.

Some, on the other hand, identify with the cracks in their heart, and define themselves by their flaws. "This is the way I am – take it or leave it."

Each of these responses leads nowhere. In the first case we try to deny the flaw; in the second case we so identify with the flaw that it becomes what we define as ourselves. In each case we effectively avoid responsibility for our lives.

There are people who have taken a third option. They have allowed themselves to descend below the crack in the heart to the heart itself. They neither cover over nor identify with the crack, but act from below it. Their words and actions have power.

The Vietnamese Bishop Francis Xavier Nguyen Van Thuan spent 13 years in prison in Vietnam, nine of them in solitary confinement. He had nothing to support him but the strength of his convictions. He was pushed to the limits of his personal resources. Many times he was brought to the brink of madness, but he managed to survive under these inhuman conditions. At first he struggled against the conditions he was living in, thinking that God was to be found somewhere in his previous life as a bishop, or in some non-existent future. A decisive moment came when he realised that God was to be found in the very conditions he was living in. He emerged, from his time of trial, a man of authenticity. The books he wrote during and after his imprisonment have a simple directness that touches the heart of any reader. After his release from prison he was invited to preach the annual retreat to the Pope and cardinals. The talks he gave were subsequently published in book form.[78] What the bishop said to the Pope and cardinals had none of the theological density that one may have expected. What he wrote came from no text-book learning or hear-say knowledge, but from somewhere deep within. The lute-player had tuned his life to be in harmony with the Word of God.

When this happens the harmonies and even the discords make good music. When the core of our being is tuned to God, the externals become less important, and what we see as struggles in our journey of faith take on a new aspect.

An earnest pilgrim in the spiritual life found himself struggling against what he saw as obstacles to coming closer to God. One day his guide said to him: "You have come to me month after month, and you talk to me about the things that are getting in the way of your progress. You tell me of your failures and your struggles. You talk to me of how others make life difficult for you. You say: 'if only this' and 'if only that' and you speak of what's in the way of your path. But you are like someone making a journey from one city to another, who finds that in front of him, blocking his path, is a range of mountains. It's no good denying that the mountains exist. It's no good standing helpless before the mountains. The way to the city is over or through the mountains. Don't think that you will find God when all your troubles are over and gone. God is in the midst of them. Don't you realise – what's *in* the way *is* the way."

Caryll Houselander

 aryll Houselander is not a particularly well-known figure today, but she is a good example of a 'normal mystic' living 'a normal mystical life'.

Born in England in 1901, she died of cancer in 1954. When she was six her mother converted to Catholicism and Caryll was also baptised. Shortly after her ninth birthday her parents separated and her mother opened a boarding house to support the family. Caryll was sent away to a convent for her education.

In her teens she returned to help her mother in the management of the boarding house. Her mother allowed a priest to stay with them and this became such a source of gossip and scandal that Caryll and her mother were ostracised by fellow-Catholics. This may have partly influenced Caryll's decision to leave the Church as a teenager, not returning until she was in her twenties.

In her early life she met and fell in love with Sidney Reilly, the famous English spy and the model for Ian Fleming's *James Bond* novels. He left her broken-hearted when he married another woman. She never married.

From early childhood Caryll seems to have been specially gifted with an insight into beauty and suffering. This insight made her writings particularly influential, especially during the bombing of

London in the Second World War. Her remarkable book, *This War is the Passion*, spoke directly to people suffering the horrors of war, showing how through suffering each person has a part to play in the redemption of the world.

This insight and compassion was no doubt enriched by three mystical experiences which happened at different periods of her life.

The first experience occurred when she was a twelve-year-old pupil at the convent school. One day she entered a room and saw a Bavarian nun sitting by herself, weeping as she polished shoes. As she stared she saw the nun's head being pressed down by a crown of thorns. She interpreted this as Christ suffering in the woman. She wrote: "I stood for – I suppose – a few seconds, dumbfounded, and then, finding my tongue, I said to her: 'I would not cry, if I was wearing the crown of thorns like you are'."

When she was 17, she received her second mystical experience. One night as she was walking down the street to do shopping, she saw what she later described as a huge Russian icon spread across the sky. She interpreted the figure as Christ on the Cross, brooding over the broken world. Shortly after this she read in a newspaper the news of the assassination of the Russian Tsar Nicholas II. The face she saw in the newspaper photograph was the face of the Christ-figure she had seen spread out over the sky.

Her third experience of Christ took place years later when she was travelling on a busy underground train. She wrote:

"I was in an underground train, a crowded train in which all sorts of people jostled together... Quite suddenly I saw with my mind, but as vividly as a wonderful picture, Christ in them all. But I saw more than that; not only was Christ in every one of them, living in them, dying in them, rejoicing in them, sorrowing in them – but because He was in them, and because they were here, the whole world was here too, here in this underground train ... I came out into the street and walked for a long time in the crowds. It was the same here, on every side, in every passerby, everywhere – Christ."

"Although (the vision) did not prevent me from ever sinning again, it showed me what sin is, especially those sins done in the name of 'love' ... I saw too the reverence that everyone must have for a sinner;

instead of condoning his sin, which is in reality his utmost sorrow,
honour must be paid even to those sinners whose souls seem to be
dead, because it is Christ, who is the life of the soul, who is dead in
them; they are His tombs, and Christ in the tomb is potentially the
risen Christ. For the same reason, no one of us who has fallen into
mortal sin himself must ever lose hope." [79]

These experiences are crucial to Caryll's spirituality. She wrote that she did not expect to find goodness in people, but "to find Christ wounded in them; and of course that is what I do find".

She had such empathy for wounded humans and such a talent for helping people to rebuild their broken worlds that during the war some doctors sent patients to her for healing. One eminent psychiatrist said of her: "She loved them back to life ... she was a divine eccentric."

Eccentric she was. For some reason, known only to her, she covered her face every day with a chalky-white substance that gave her the kind of dead-white face that a friend described as "the tragic look one associates with clowns and great comedians".

The Church will probably never see Caryll Houselander canonised as a saint. She was a bit too much of this world. She swore, had a biting sense of humour, liked gin, and her habit of chain-smoking had left her "with a dandelion-yellow upper lip". And by all accounts, she didn't suffer fools gladly or even tactfully.

But today she is being quietly re-discovered as a woman whose spiritual experiences gave her an insight into Christ's suffering at the heart of the world. Far from making her writings heavy with pain, this insight gave her a joyful view. Her writings have a musical quality to them. This is clear in her comment on The Wedding Feast of Cana:

"It is a delight to think that this first miracle was in no way connect-
ed with unhappiness. It was not healing sickness, forgiving sins, or
raising the dead; it was simply giving joy, more joy, to people who
were already rejoicing." [80]

THE REED

Emptiness is the beginning of contemplation.

It is not a fruitless emptiness, a void without a meaning; on the contrary, it has a shape, a form given to it by the purpose for which it is intended.

It is the emptiness like the hollow in the reed, the narrow riftless emptiness which can have only one destiny: to receive the piper's breath and utter the song that is in his heart.

It is the emptiness like the hollow in the cup, shaped to receive water or wine.

It is the emptiness like that of the bird's nest built in a round warm ring to receive the little bird.

Caryll Houselander, Emptiness

Playing the song in the singer's heart

When James Galway plays the flute, the sound is unmistakable. I can almost always recognise that tone or style, whether he's playing classical music of Mozart, Bach and Vivaldi, or light music, Irish traditional music, or music from the sound track of *The Lord of the Rings*. There's something unique about the tone and quality of the flute he plays.

I had always thought this was because he had a flute made of silver. But on looking at his website, I discovered that he not only had a flute of silver, but one of gold, one of platinum and a collection of many others which he would turn to from time to time to suit his mood or the style of music he was playing. On a video clip he plays one piece of music on 16 different flutes, and invites his viewers to notice the difference between each instrument. There is a perceptible difference between each one: the tone, the quality of sound, the pitch – all these are slightly different. It made me realise how much the quality of an instrument affects the music played. What made me consider this further was a comment that he wrote in a letter to an enquirer. He said that his wife Jeanne – herself a concert flautist – thought that when he played on a gold flute, it reflected better on his mature personality. He wrote: "My wife Jeanne has been listening to me play the flute for nearly every day for the last 22 years or more. She thinks I sound the best on gold, but that the other metals have different qualities. She told me gold sounds warmer and thinks that I sound like a young James Galway when I play on silver."

There's a lot in that comment. The temperament and mood of the artist plays a big part in how music sounds. When the quality of the musical instrument fits with and reflects the temperament of the artist, the music springs to life. The clear, light, almost piercing sound of James Galway's silver flute suited and reflected the young Galway with his bushy dark beard, his twinkling eyes and his close-to-the-surface humour. I'm sure he used his silver flute when he played the *Bandinerie* from Bach's suite No 2, or when he gave his lightning-fast virtuoso rendition of *The Flight of the Bumble Bee*. But when he played the reflective *Annie's Song* or the somewhat mystical score from *The Lord of the Rings* it might well have been a flute of another make that he used.

The point is that good music depends on the genius of the composer and the skill and the temperament of the performer, but the quality of the musical instrument also plays a crucial part in bringing the best out of good music. When the instrument is "just the right instrument", it brings together all the other elements of quality music.

Caryll Houselander's book, *The Reed of God*, from which the image of the reed comes, is a reflection on the life of Mary, the mother of Jesus. Although whole chapters in the book make no reference to her, the book is an extended meditation on Mary as "just the right instrument" in the hands of God. It's a beautiful image to use of the woman whose life began with a song of praise and whose womb became the hollow nest in which the Son of God grew. Mary was the instrument which God could best use for the first chapter in the drama of the salvation of mankind. She was a reed hollowed out and ready for the breath of the Holy Spirit, hollow and open "to receive the piper's breath and utter the song that is in his heart. "

Caryll Houselander described Mary as an "ordinary person". She wrote:

> "A very great many people still think of Mary as someone who would never do anything that we do. To many she is the Madonna of the Christmas card, immobile, seated forever in the immaculately clean stable of golden straw and shining snow. She is not real; nothing about her is real, not even the stable in which Love was born ... The one thing that she did and does is the one thing that we all have to do, namely to bear Christ into the world."

When Houselander wrote those words in the 1950s, she would have surprised and even shocked some Catholic Christians who preferred to see Mary as extraordinary. But she was right. Mary was an ordinary person because she was herself, and she was everything that God wanted her to be when creating her: a perfectly tuned and toned instrument of human nature.

But in fact, "being ordinary" is actually very extraordinary, and most of us find it very difficult. Being oneself, accepting oneself, being the sort of person one is made to be, is one of the hardest tasks we face throughout our lives. Most of us secretly long to be something or someone other than we are.

A flute is made to produce certain sounds. If a flute could speak, it may be tempted to say things like: "Why can't I make a crashing sound like the drums?" or "Why do I have such a small part to play in the orchestra?" But anyone can see that these are foolish questions. The flute's job is to be a flute, and the better the flute is, the better the sound that comes from it. No two flutes make exactly the same sound, and no two people are created to make the same contribution to life. Each one of us is created to make a unique contribution that no other human being will ever make. Our task is to be what we were made to be, nothing more and nothing less; but to be that with passion, and to do all we can to become the best of what we were made to be.

The composer Arthur Sullivan dreamed all his life of writing a grand oratorio and becoming famous for what people thought was 'serious music'. It took him a long time to realise that the music he wrote for the scripts of William Gilbert was his great contribution to the world. He will always be known as the composer of the Gilbert and Sullivan operettas.

Hans Christian Andersen wanted to write great epic poems. But he brought joy to people in almost every country in the world for his fairy tales. He recognised this at the end of his life, and found deep peace. At his death he wrote: "To God and man, my thanks, my love."

One thing that prevents us from being fully ourselves is the idea that somehow our 'human life' and our 'spiritual life' are two different and separate – and sometimes contradictory – things. Caryll Houselander often spoke out against a lack of connection between religion and life. She wrote:

> "There are many people in the world who cultivate a curious state which they call 'the spiritual life'. They often complain that they have very little time to devote to this 'spiritual' life. The only time they do not regard as wasted is the time they can devote to pious exercises: praying, reading, meditations, and visiting the Church. All the time spent in earning a living, cleaning the home, caring for the children, making and mending clothes, cooking, and all the other manifold

duties and responsibilities, is regarded as wasted. Yet it is really through ordinary human life and the things of every hour of every day that union comes about."

That's the key. It is through ordinary human life and in the things of every hour of every day that we find our God. And union with God, or contemplation, which so many people think is the special prerogative of enclosed monks and nuns, is actually what we are all called to. Whoever we are, whatever we do, we shouldn't be afraid to recognise that contemplation is something we all do, often without being conscious of it. But to be conscious of it is to raise it to a level which profoundly affects our lives.

The image of the reed helps us to recognise the two actions involved in developing the art and habit of contemplation. There's the action of God, who in various ways whittles away at our insides, cutting away the stuff in us that might block the breath of the Spirit, creating a hollow space where the sound of God's music can echo. And then there is the action of ourselves, who actively collaborate in God's action, even when we don't understand, don't like and don't find it easy what God seems to be doing with us.

I have often seen this happening in people's lives. I have seen people whose lives have been marked by this painful process of being emptied and hollowed out by God. They may have faced hurts and disillusionments as children and young people. They may have had to struggle with a marriage which hasn't turned out as they had hoped. Or perhaps they've had to cope with debilitating sickness, or even perhaps the tragic death of their own children. Or maybe they have had to face some form of shame and public humiliation. I've watched as they have struggled to accept these things that have chiselled away at their very interior, and I've had to accept my own inability to find the right words to help them or encourage them.

But so often I am lost in admiration at what I see with the passage of time: people who have grown in inner beauty, who have found a deep peace, an inner equilibrium, a tranquillity of spirit, and in the end the capacity to "see all things in God and God in all things". They are the real contemplatives in the world. They have become instruments playing the music of God. They have come to live fully their ordinary lives and they have come to recognise that it is *in this world*, and in the life that they have been given, that they will find and recognise the God with whom they will spend eternity.

This is why the true mystics, the true contemplatives, were people who loved the world. There are so many examples of these people. The most obvious to us all, of course, is St Francis of Assisi, who celebrated the beauty of creation with such ecstatic praise; who called the sun his brother and the moon his sister; whose love for animals enabled him to talk to the birds and to tame wild beasts; who presented the world with the Christmas crib to remind us of the wonder of God becoming a human being; and who at the end of his life welcomed death as his sister and called the earth of his grave his friend.

Caryll Houselander loved life, and clung to it with vigour. She reveals this in a letter she wrote as she struggled with her terminal cancer. To a woman she was helping through depression she wrote: "I agree with you about the 'importance of living'. I go further: it seems to me that the very great thing is to be able to enjoy life." She saw her life as a song, and in the middle of her last illness, she wrote: "I honestly long to be told 'a hundred percent cure' and to return to this life to celebrate it with gramophone records, giggling and gin."

It was here in the world she loved that she discovered her God, and she discovered God's plan for her in all her eccentricity and brokenness. The plan of God for us all is this: a song of love. We don't write the music, and we are not the players of the music. The song is the song of God's love. The musician is Jesus. We are the instruments in the hands of the divine musician. For better or for worse.

Hildegarde of Bingen

or nearly 800 years and up to recent times, Hildegard of Bingen has been unknown outside of the small group of her followers. And yet at the time of her death she was regarded as one of the greatest women of her century. She was a Benedictine nun, a mystic, a poet, an artist, musician and effective administrator. She wrote books on natural phenomena and she discovered natural remedies for illnesses; she wrote books on theology and wrote commentaries on Scripture; she wrote liturgical and sacred music; and she composed musical plays on spiritual themes. Though not officially canonised as a saint by the Church, she is recognised as such by popular acclaim in some parts of the Church.

Her writings were read by Pope Eugenius to the assembled bishops at the Synod of Trier. She preached in churches, monasteries and convents. She spoke to bishops and princes, and on one occasion addressed the emperor Frederick Barbarossa and his court. She didn't hesitate to ask the clergy to reform their disordered way of life.

Her life spans a good part of the twelfth century, a century which was filled with conflicts and religious restlessness. She was born in 1098 and died in 1179. From a very early age she was gifted with exceptional natural and spiritual gifts, and even as a young woman she received visions which she later wrote down in a book called

Scivias – Know the ways of the Lord. This book not only contained her recollection of visions, but in time evolved into a theological work dealing with the theology of creation and redemption. It was the first of what was to become a trilogy of works of deep theological significance.

As a young child Hildegard was offered to God by her parents as a child oblate. She was placed in the care of a relative named Jutta who lived nearby as a hermit. In time this hermitage developed into a Benedictine community. Hildegard received the habit as a Benedictine at the age of 15 and for the next 17 years lived a strictly enclosed life. In 1136 she was elected abbess of the convent and a few years later she moved the convent to Rupertsberg in the Rhine valley near Bingen.

At the age of 42, Hildegard had a powerful prophetic vision in which she experienced God as the "living light". She wrote of this vision:

> *"And it came to pass ... when I was 42 years and 7 months old, that the heavens were opened and a blinding light of exceptional brilliance flowed through my entire brain. And so it kindled my whole heart and breast like a flame, not burning but warming ...and suddenly I understood the meaning of Scripture, namely the Psalter, the Gospels and the other catholic volumes of both the Old and New Testaments."*

Hildegard hesitated to act, overwhelmed by feelings of inadequacy:

> *"But although I heard and saw these things, because of doubt and low opinion of myself and because of diverse sayings of men, I refused for a long time a call to write, not out of stubbornness but out of humility, until weighed down by a scourge of God, I fell onto a bed of sickness."*

On regaining her health she began a period of intense creative writing and administrative activity as she built up the life of her community at Rupertsberg.

In one of her visions she heard a voice commanding her to:

> *"Arise, therefore, cry out and tell what is shown to you by the strong power of God's help. God who rules all of creation with power and mercy floods those who fear Him and serve Him with joyous love and humility with the light of celestial illumination."* (Scivias 1,1)

At the age of 60, and despite her ill health, she set out to communicate her message beyond the convent. She travelled throughout southern Germany and into Switzerland and as far as Paris, carrying out her mission to "teach, preach, interpret the scripture and proclaim the justice of God" to people of all classes and vocations. She spoke to peasants, priests, monks, bishops, nuns, princes and political leaders.

Five years later she returned to her convent and she wrote her second great theological work, *The Book of Divine Merits*. This book grew out of her experience as a spiritual guide. She then wrote the third book in her trilogy, *The Book of Divine Works*. This book is a commentary on the Prologue of St John's Gospel and on the first chapter of the book of Genesis.

Hildegard's theology is deeply authentic and truly feminine in its approach. She sees creation as a network of connected elements. The cosmos is God's dwelling and our home. The goal of creation is to be a harmonious, interrelated web of life in which every element of creation finds its place in peace and harmony. The effect of the sin of Adam and Eve was to put humanity into a state of cracked relationships and disharmony, where humankind's relationship to the body, to nature, to others and to God has been distorted. Faced with this state of exile and alienation, humankind should not despair, because humanity has the potential to reconnect. Our deep desire for God is part of our true nature and potential.

Hildegard had a great love for the Church, and like Catherine of Siena two centuries later, she felt deeply the wounds of the Church and its need to reform. This desire for reform, along with her strong personality, brought her into conflict with authorities in the Church.

In her lifetime Hildegard was known as "the Sybil of the Rhine" because of her many gifts: music, song and poetry. She died on 17 September 1179. Her surviving works include more than 100 letters to emperors and popes, bishops, nuns and nobility. She wrote 72 songs including a play set to music. Hildegard has undergone a remarkable rise in popularity in the last 30 years.

THE FEATHER FLOATING FREELY

Listen: There was once a King sitting on his throne. Around him stood great and wonderfully beautiful columns ornamented with ivory, bearing the banners of the King with great honour. Then it pleased the King to raise a small feather from the ground, and he commanded it to fly. The feather flew, not because of anything in itself, but because the air bore it along. This am I.

Hildegarde of Bingen, *Selected Writings*

LIVING MORE FREELY, MORE FLOWINGLY

It is never a happy thing to watch the marriage of friends unravel and come to an end. So much time, so many hopes and dreams shared at the beginning, so many memories, and now...

When two friends of mine separated I could see what was happening, but could do nothing to help them in what was drawing to an inevitable conclusion. What had initially brought them together – complementary qualities – had now become a wedge which drove them apart.

He was strong, determined, an achiever, reliable and a great provider. She was a free-floating character, sensitive, and a softening element in the relationship. They were drawn to each other by the qualities they recognised that they lacked in themselves.

I remember listening while she told me of a significant conversation they had shared. She had said to him: "You know, you so often come home from work and you tell me what a hard time you had during the day. You tell me how you solved this or that problem; how you managed to rescue a situation from becoming disastrous; how this or that person was not up to his job; how you brought things to a successful conclusion. But you've never come home and said: 'I blew it; I said the wrong thing; I didn't know what to do in that situation; I really don't know what to do next ...'" He was horrified. "But of course," he said, "how could I come home and say that I didn't know what to do, that I had failed, that I had dropped the pass, that I had missed a chance? You would have lost respect for me!" "Not at all," she replied, "I would have loved you more."

There's a beauty in strength, certainly. But there's a beauty in vulnerability, a different beauty, perhaps, but a powerful one, especially when that vulnerability reflects or creates an inner freedom. Hildegarde captures this in her image. On the one hand there is the royal palace, the king sitting on his throne surrounded by beautiful, strong and ornate columns, with banners carrying symbols of the king's authority and power. But then there's the picture of the delicate feather wafting and floating in the breeze in this vast hall of the palace.

Hildegarde's image is not so much a description of the power of the Holy Spirit. It's a description of the vulnerable Christian person who freely and consciously allows the Spirit to take the lead. "This am I," says Hildegarde in three telling words as she reflects on the feather. The fragility of the vulnerable feather seems more powerful than the grandeur of the palace of the king. One can almost imagine the courtiers standing round in this immense hall, gazing with fascination at the delicate beauty of the feather floating in the breeze.

This interplay of vulnerability and inner freedom, which is such a part of the Christian mystery, was reflected in a remarkable way in the life of Etty Hillesum, a young Dutch woman, Jewish by birth but brought up without any religious faith during the most horrific years of Jewish persecution by the Nazis in the Second World War. She had all the marks of a mystic, yet almost everything in her life was not what we would call 'conventional'. Her family life was unconventional. She had no conventional religious practice, her political stance was abnormal, and her early emotional and sexual life was tempestuous. She died at the age of 29 in the death camp of Auschwitz, where her parents and one of her brothers also perished. The world has only discovered her in recent years. It would never have heard of her but for the remarkable diaries she left behind.

Etty was born in 1914 into a family that would be described today as 'dysfunctional'. Her parents' marriage was uneasy and strained. Her father was an excellent, disciplined scholar; her mother was passionate and chaotic. In fact, the word Etty used most when depicting her family life was "chaos". She had two brothers, both of whom were brilliant; both suffered psychological problems and spent time in psychiatric institutions. Etty herself experienced great emotional instability and suffered severe bouts of depression. She studied and graduated with a degree in Law.

In March 1937, at the age of 23, Etty boarded in the house of an accountant, Hendrik Wegerif, a widower aged 62, who hired her as a housekeeper. They became lovers. Etty stayed in this house till 1943, the year she made the journey to her death in Auschwitz.

Etty's most significant relationship was with the psychochirologist, Julius Spier. Spier had worked in Zurich with the psychoanalyst Carl Jung, who had encouraged him to develop his skills in chirology, the practice of psychoanalysis through reading people's palms. He was a gifted and charismatic figure and gathered round him a group of students, among whom was Etty. She became his assistant, his intellectual partner, friend and lover.

Etty began a course in therapy with Spier, and immediately began writing her diary. The opening words of her first entry will attract any reader. She wrote: "Here goes, then." She then goes on to reveal her commitment to the inner work of self-knowledge. "The main difficulty, I think, is a sense of shame. So many inhibitions, so much fear of letting go, of allowing things to pour out of me, and yet that is what I must do if I am ever to give my life a reasonable and satisfying purpose."

The course of her inner transformation is traced out in the eight exercise books full of entries covering a period of two and a half years. During this time she lived in Camp Westerbork, in the north-eastern Netherlands. This camp was the last stop for more than 100,000 Dutch Jews en route to Auschwitz and other Nazi extermination camps. In the camp she poured out her life for those detained there as they waited for their inevitable final journey. In her own remarkable words she described herself as "the thinking heart of the barracks".

And while this outpouring of her life was going on in the camp, her inner self was being transformed from hatred to love, from resentment to forgiveness, from despair to hope, and finally to an inner freedom that nothing could restrain.

Etty discovered God, learned to call on the name of God, and she began to learn the art of praying. In one of the entries in her diary she writes: "What a strange story it is, my story: the girl who could not kneel. Or its variation: the girl who learned to pray. That is my most intimate gesture, more intimate even than being with a man."

She wrote from the camp on August 18 1943: "My life has become an uninterrupted dialogue with You, O God, one great dialogue."

The remarkable thing was that this inner transformation to a sense of freedom took place in one of the darkest and most tragic periods of human history. What was happening inside her was liberation and life; what was happening all around her was captivity and extermination.

Finally, she herself joined those who made the final journey to death. With her two parents and one of her brothers, she was put on a train bound for Auschwitz. Etty's parents either died on the voyage, or were gassed immediately on arrival. Etty died on November 30, 1943. Her older brother died in Auschwitz the following year. Her younger brother died on the journey from the extermination camp in Bergen-Belsen when it was partially evacuated in 1945.

The last words we have of Etty were written on the day that she left for Auschwitz. Before the deportees finally left the Netherlands, Etty threw a postcard out of the window of the train. It was addressed to a friend, and the message read: "We left the camp singing." From the core of her being she discovered a way to find song in the midst of a chaotic life, in a world surrounded by evidence of the most inhuman cruelty.

Etty Hillesum's writings are unconventional, as was her life. She was a living witness to the fact that God does not work within the confines and categories that we might expect: conventions of faith, religious practice, moral conduct, forms of worship and ways of prayer. God too is unconventional. And Etty was a witness to what it means to be vulnerable and yet free to move and be moved at the breath of the Spirit of God.

She lived with the ambiguities and even contradictions in her own life, and accepted those ambiguities in the world around her.

The early pages of her diary reveal an emotionally disturbed and sexually disordered young woman struggling with an inner life that she cannot understand. In her first entry in her diary, March 9 1941, the 27-year-old Etty described herself as one who was "accomplished in bed, just about seasoned enough I should think to be counted among the better lovers, and love does indeed suit me to perfection, yet it remains a mere trifle, set apart from what is truly essential, and deep inside me something is still locked away".

Her relationship with Julius Spier was at once erotic and spiritual. She sees no contradiction between the two. Paradoxically, her relationship with Spier, alongside her intimate relationship with Wegerif, helped her to develop a deep religious sensibility. It was Spier who helped her to speak the name of God without embarrassment, and it was he who invited her to make the journey inwards to discover the presence of God in her deepest self.

This deep self she likened to a hidden spring, a well which often enough is blocked. "There is a deep well inside me. And in it dwells God. Sometimes I am there, too. But more often stones and grit block the well, and God is buried beneath. Then he must be dug out again."

The journey of her transformation is framed by two statements she makes in her diary which act like book-ends to the process of her inner discovery. In the opening pages of her diary she writes: "deep down something like a tightly-wound ball of twine binds me relentlessly", and yet later she could write: "Suddenly I was living differently, more freely, more flowingly." In between those two statements there are others which describe her turbulent confusions. In one entry she reflects: "I know again now that I am not mad. I simply need to do a lot of work on myself before I develop into an adult and a complete human being."

We will never know what required of Etty the greatest courage: facing the evil and darkness in the world outside her, or facing the confusion and darkness within, or letting herself go and be taken by the breath of God beyond the boundaries of her life. What we do learn from her diaries is that she did all three of these. She wrote: "I have looked our destruction, our miserable end... straight in the eye, and accepted it into my life. And my love of life has not been diminished." That's the thing that sets her apart from others. Her love of life was not diminished, and she ended her life singing.

Though our path to inner wholeness will not be like Etty's, there does come a moment when we, like her, come face-to-face with the contradictions and ambiguities of our inner life. We are always a work-in-progress, which is a most uncomfortable situation to be in. We usually judge what is happening to us as we slide from one chaotic moment to another as a sign that we are slipping out of the hands of God. It might be precisely at that moment that we are most surely and firmly in the hands of God. It may be that we are being gently wafted by the power of the Spirit.

Teresa of Avila

ne of the delights for any tourist in Rome is that one can walk almost anywhere and find, in unexpected places, treasures of art or architecture that would be considered priceless anywhere in the world. On the side of a not-too-frequently used street in Rome is a little church, not much different from the other 904 churches in the city. Inside, the light is dim, and one could easily miss a precious piece of work by Bernini, tucked away on the left hand side of the church. It depicts the Transverberation of St Teresa, an incident in the life of St Teresa of Avila, when, after a series of intense visions, Teresa's heart was, as it were, pierced with a spear by Jesus, symbolising her union with Him and the suffering that this would cost. This is what the mystics call the state of "mystical marriage". The sculpture is a masterpiece, and Bernini adds a human – almost comical – touch to the work. On either side of the piece he has carved a number of people, presumably friends or members of his family, sitting in viewing boxes, watching the experience as if it were an opera!

That part is not factual, but Teresa's experience is. It took place in 1559, twenty-three years before she died. St Teresa is one of the greatest mystics the Church has known, and, perhaps because of this, most of us are inclined to see her as someone who was formed from an early age into the highest stages of prayer.

But she didn't begin this way. She was a spirited woman, and in real prayer she was a late starter. She came from an affluent family from the Spanish city of Avila. She was one of 12 children, and when she was only seven she ran away from home with her little brother to seek martyrdom at the hands of the Moors. When Teresa was only 13 years old, her mother died. Teresa was a pleasure-loving girl, and her father sent her to a convent 'finishing school'.

At the age of 21 Teresa entered the Carmelite convent of the Incarnation just outside the city, joining a community of 150 nuns. In her autobiography, Teresa writes that she was afraid of marriage. That may have been one of her motives for entering the convent, but she also admits that she was not fired by great love of God in doing so. She herself writes that her first 20 years in the convent were what she called "20 years on a stormy sea". The stormy sea was a life of flippancy and superficiality on the one hand, and on the other a struggle with some alarming illnesses. For these years Teresa always prayed from a book, and one of her prayer books is still preserved in the convent. Its pages are yellow and dog-eared, and it is heavily marked. But prayer was hard for Teresa. She tells us that she would often spend the time of prayer watching the hands of the clock. For a year she gave up even trying to meditate.

But then, at the age of 40, a change took place. Teresa began to have visions "with the eyes of her soul" and to hear through her "inward ear" voices speaking to her. She feared that she was deluding herself. Some of her directors were *sure* she was deluding herself. But she found good guidance from three priests, two of whom were later canonised: St Francis Borgia, St Peter of Alcantara and Balthazar Alvarez. With their encouragement, she pressed on with her inner journey.

This journey led her to become one of the greatest mystics and at the same time one of the greatest reforming figures in Catholic history.

It's difficult to know what is more remarkable about Teresa: the extraordinary graces of prayer granted to her by God, or her tireless energy in reforming and refounding convents. Perhaps the two things are just two sides of the same coin. She journeyed round those convents in an old, lumbering, covered wagon, sleeping in bug-infested inns on very cold nights. At the same time she was also writing prodigiously. She said once: "I wish I could write with both hands, so as not to forget one thing while I'm saying another." She had a mission, and having once known the touch of God, there was nothing that would stop her on that mission, not even the severe criticism that she had to suffer. A papal nuncio, one of her many opponents, called her "a restless, disobedient, contumacious gadabout". But Teresa knew what it meant to be changed by the love of God. She knew, too, the hesitation that we so often feel at the outset of our journey to the Lord. From personal experience she knew that the only fear greater than the fear of asking God to set us free is the fear that this may actually happen!

Teresa knew what it meant to let go of one life and emerge into another. Her famous book, *The Interior Castle*, describes the spiritual voyage as a journey through the doors of a mansion: one door leads to another, and another and another. Then we realise that this castle is actually within each one of us, and as we emerge from it, we enter into the everyday world to which we belong, but with a transformed view of reality.

Teresa's writing is full of wonderful images, but the image of the butterfly emerging from its cocoon is one of her best. It helps us to see the really human side of Teresa, and brings home to us again the truth that while God has made us, loves us and keeps us as we are, God also invites us to a life that is different, fuller, richer and more glorious – if we want it.

THE BUTTERFLY

You must have already heard about God's marvels manifested in the way silk originates, for only God could have invented something like that. The silkworms come from seeds about the size of little grains of pepper. When the warm weather comes and the leaves begin to appear on the mulberry tree, the seeds start to live, for they are dead until then. The worms nourish themselves on the mulberry leaves until, having grown to full size, they settle on some twigs. Then with their little mouths, they themselves go about spinning the silk and making some very thick little cocoons in which they enclose themselves. The silkworm, which is fat and ugly, then dies, and a little white butterfly, which is very pretty, comes forth from the cocoon.

Teresa of Avila, The Interior Castle

"When you're dead, you're dead for life!"

Medical experts have written about the amazing capacity of the human body to revive and heal itself. People who are familiar with the inner life of the spirit know that the inner spirit of each person has the same remarkable capacity for new life. As each of us goes through the storms and deserts of life, we are challenged to let go of something we think is important and even essential to our existence. Loss of health, loss of security, loss of marriage partner, loss of job or home, loss of strength, loss of youth or innocence or virtue – these are all moments which bring confusion, pain and anxiety. Often we feel alone in a world that's collapsing all around us. It's hard to see that this moment of 'death' may be the moment when something new is about to be born.

But from the very depths of our being a healing process begins. Where this healing power comes from is a mystery; but either at the time, or as we look back, we begin to realise that a door has opened where we thought we could see only a wall.

The image of the butterfly emerging from its cocoon represents for many people just this experience of new life emerging. As with the transformed state of the butterfly, this new life is fresh and beautiful, but fragile. It appears just when the cocoon of darkness appears to be our only state, or just when we have found comfort in remaining in a state which we think is our place of security. The butterfly is a wonderful symbol of hope whose seed-bed is pain; a symbol of the spring of new life which flows quietly but inexorably within us, and which breaks forth at the moment of deepest crisis.

In the middle of her image, Teresa brings a homely touch as she admits her ignorance when talking of the silk worm. She says: "I have never seen this, but I've heard of it, and so if something in the explanation gets distorted, it won't be my fault." In fact she does confuse moths and butterflies, but her image is valid: the picture of new life emerging from what appears to be a death. But the process is not an automatic one. It involves a delicate balance of active cooperation and simple waiting. Teresa likens the mulberry leaves to the Word of God, which we feed on to make us strong. Then building the cocoon takes effort, as does the patience in waiting for the moment when God sets us free into a new life. She concludes: "Look at the difference between an ugly worm and a little white butterfly: that's what the difference is here."

It seems easy when you read all this on paper, and in times of tranquillity and calm all of us can see the spiritual logic in "letting go and letting God". We can even think of examples in the lives of others when this process of going from death to new life was so obviously a part of God's plan for them. The problem always comes when *we* are invited to enter the process! But there's nothing more likely than that we *will* be invited to make this journey.

Take the human experience of displacement, for example. Displacement is the experience of being moved from what is considered to be an ordinary and proper place. Things are displaced when they get lost or are left in places which are not their normal and appropriate homes. But the same can be said of human experiences. We spend a good part of our energy and time creating surroundings that become 'normal and proper' for us: a routine of life, a group of friends, a place for living. These become our roots, which give us the security to grow. Life would be unnecessarily difficult if every day started completely new and we had to decide at every moment what was to happen next. But then, when these 'normal and proper' surroundings are removed, we experience a sense of displacement. Though these experiences are part of life, they take their toll, and often require an adjustment like the death/life process of the silkworm. We leave school and have to adjust to a new world of relationships and responsibilities. We fail a crucial examination. We marry and find our lives changing radically, and changing again as a family grows. We move from one home to another. We change – or lose – our job. We watch while our children leave home. We let go of relationships and try to establish new ones. We see the death of a partner. We try to adapt to new surroundings or a new culture. We pass inevitably from childhood to adolescence, and to maturity and old age.

Life is a constant flow of these displacement experiences. They don't automatically lead to the new life of the butterfly state, and sometimes people don't manage the struggle that's involved in crossing from one state to another. Libraries are full of books on the difficulties and pitfalls that lie before us on our journey through life. We've all met people who have been unable to make the adjustments successfully. We know people who have not been able to establish new relationships, or to settle in a place which is different. We know people who have not let go of their adolescence or childhood, or who have not adjusted to the new situation they find themselves in.

If we can manage the transition we understand the death that's involved in the change to a new state. But at the same time we begin to experience the new life that this transition gives. What used to give life and energy is now seen from a different perspective. The new experience has expanded us, and we realise that there is much more to life than we had thought. We feel grateful that we decided – or were forced – not to stay in the rut, even though it may have cost us an internal bruising.

But experiences of displacement can strike us at an even deeper, and often more painful and confusing level, the level of our spirit. At this level we are being touched at the very depth of our being, at the level of things we hold most dearly: our certainties in life, our value system, our assurance of faith, our understanding of God and our relationship with God. What a death experience takes place when we are forced to question even these most sacred things!

Let us for a moment draw alongside those two disillusioned disciples of Jesus as they walked to Emmaus. Here, if ever, was a situation of displacement of spirit. As a group oppressed by Roman authority, and longing for a messiah to lead them to victory with or without bloodshed, they had interpreted Jesus' words as confirming their hopes for a political messiah who would free them from this rule. They had put their hopes in Jesus. They may even have thought that at the last moment something dramatic might happen from the cross. But nothing. Jesus was really dead. As dead as he could possibly be. And when the mysterious stranger drew near to these men, they openly confessed their disillusionment. Everything they had believed, all their values, all their hopes, had been thrown into confusion. "We had hoped that he might set Israel free," they said, "but now our leaders had him crucified... And this is not all. Two whole days have gone by since it all happened." "We had hoped ... But now... And that is not all..." Like hammer blows, these phrases punctuate the disciples' conversation, and poignantly sum up the descent into disappointment and disillusionment those men experienced. The very foundations of their lives were shaken. They had reached rock-bottom.

When we experience moments of spiritual displacement, these are the same words we use to describe how we feel. "I had hoped ... But now... And that is not all..." How is it possible for one whose only hope and dream for marriage was to be a good partner and parent to believe that new life may come from the breakdown of that marriage? How is it possible for parents to sit by the deathbed of an only child and believe that they may find a new life from this tragedy? How is it possible for a young person to hope for a new life when the only person in his or her life has walked out of the relationship? How is it possible for parents to believe that their teenage children may actually be called to a new relationship with God as they reject and leave behind the expressions of faith that their parents had so carefully tried to pass on to them? How is it possible for you or for me to believe that there can be new life for us when some dark secret we have been carrying for a long time is brought to light, and we are left exposed, naked, vulnerable, and ashamed?

It is then that the mysterious Stranger wants to draw near and open our eyes, as he did to the disciples. "Of course! Wasn't it part of the story that he should die and then rise again?" The disciples then learned to recognise the Lord's presence in their spiritual displacement, and another Christian paradox emerges: it is not life that comes before death, but death that comes before life. Somehow, the mystery of God is there in these profound experiences of human desolation and death, and it is all reflected in the pattern of nature. Teresa's image of the butterfly challenges the very basis of our belief, but gives us hope at the same time.

This is how Jesus understood the 'conversion' to which he invites us. For him, conversion is not so much a call to penitential exercises or confession of sin, but primarily an invitation to change our perspective on life. He invites us to allow ourselves to let go of some of the ways of living that we've taken for granted, to let go of some of the things we thought were most certain, and to trust that we shall emerge to a new freedom, a new life that we never thought was possible. It's a risk that costs no less than everything. If silk-worms could think or decide, how many of them would risk entering into a cocoon, believing that they would emerge as a butterfly?

The biggest moment of transformation for us all is that final moment of our life on earth when we are called to emerge from this life to another life of which we know nothing.

I have watched in awe at the bedside of people who have made that ultimate journey across the dark threshold of life into the next. Here, in this most dramatic of moments, all are reduced to the same frail humanity – the important people of this world and the unimportant people of this world; women and men of great faith or of little faith; men and women of deep insight or of simple understanding; frail elderly people or bewildered teenagers. At this moment each one is stripped of the securities they may have used to help them through life. Now they stand alone at the threshold. Some have passed quietly and easily into that unknown world. Others have struggled, until one can sense the moment when with a sigh they let go, and enter into what they finally discover is their normal and proper place. The butterfly emerges, and I return home, wondering, and repeating that prayer of faith: "For your faithful people, life is changed, not ended."

An American poet observed two little boys playing Cowboys and Indians. One little boy wouldn't lie still after he had been 'shot'. The other, exasperated, said: "Yeah, when you're really dead, you're dead for life."

Could such profound truth be said any more simply than this?

John of the Cross

 young man of 35 emerged from a prison cell clutching a small sheaf of papers, poems he had written while in prison. The prison cell was a little room originally intended as a closet, six feet wide and ten feet long. It had no window. The only opening was a slit high up in the wall, and it was impossible to see out of it. The cell was freezing in the winter and suffocating in the summer, and the man spent nine months in these conditions.

This was no ordinary situation, because the man who emerged from this cell in 1578 was Juan de Yepes, known to us as St John of the Cross; the prison cell was a cell of his Order of Carmelites, and the small sheaf of papers were to be recognised as among the greatest pieces of Christian mystical literature. All this, written from a prison cell!

Historians suggest that there have been three great periods of mysticism in the history of the Christian Church: the third and fourth centuries in the East (Egypt, Palestine, Syria and Asia Minor); the fourteenth century in England and Northern Europe; and the sixteenth century in Spain. John of the Cross is among a group of mystics who lived in Spain in this third period, and he is one of the three who emerge as towering mystical giants of Spanish origin. The other two are Teresa of Avila and Ignatius of Loyola.

John was born in 1542, into a Jewish convert family in a small community near Avila. His father, who was disowned by his wealthy family for marrying a humble silk-weaver, died shortly after the birth of John, their third son. John, his two brothers and his widowed mother lived a life of poverty, moving around and living in various villages in the area.

At the age of 21 John entered the Carmelite monastery in Medina, later enrolling in the University of Salamanca, and was ordained a priest in 1567. While he was in Medina to celebrate his first Mass, he met Teresa of Avila, who had begun her reform within the Carmelite order. John told her that in fact he was longing for a life of deeper solitude and prayer, and had been thinking of transferring to the Carthusian Order. He was interested in helping Teresa in her plan to reform the Order, but only on the condition that he would not have to wait too long to begin. So began the link between these two extraordinary personalities. John was 25 years old, and Teresa was 52.

Of course, one accepts the vocation of reforming oneself and others only at one's own peril, and understandably; as the reform movement gathered momentum, so did resistance and opposition to both Teresa and John of the Cross. In 1577 some Carmelites seized John and demanded a renunciation of the reform. John refused. He was declared a rebel and sent to prison in the monastery in Toledo.

'Prisons' or places of confinement were not uncommon in religious monasteries in those days. Men and women may have been less committed to the religious life, or they may have needed more 'encouragement' to persevere than perhaps today. Or maybe it was just the climate of the times. Whatever the situation, imprisonment was not uncommon. What was uncommon, though, was the length of time John was imprisoned, and the severity of his punishment. His food was bread, sardines and water. Three evenings a week he had to eat kneeling on the floor in the middle of the refectory. Then, when the community had finished eating, John's shoulders were bared and each member of the community struck him with a lash while Psalm 50 was being recited. The wounds he received remained unhealed for years afterwards. After six months of this, John was assigned a new warder who was more compassionate. This warder gave him a change of clothes, and some paper and ink. John began to write down the great poems that had been forming in his mind.

It is remarkable enough that John was favoured by some of the most extraordinary mystical graces during his life. But it is equally remarkable that from conditions as appalling as his, he was able to pen poems of such intense love and freedom of spirit. Consider these lines, for example:

"One dark night
Fired with love's urgent longings
– Ah! The sheer grace! –
I went out unseen.
My house being now all stilled.

On that glad night
In secret, for no one saw me
Nor did I look at anything
With no other light or guide
Than the one that burned in my heart...."

John was to find physical freedom when he escaped from his prison in August 1578 and journeyed to southern Spain. The following years were spent in administration and in writing commentaries on his poems. His troubles were not over, however. He was again accused of disturbing the order, and in 1591 he was again sent to a solitary monastery in southern Spain, and while there, he learned of efforts being made to expel him even from the reform movement which he had initiated.

In that same year, he succumbed to a fever, and he was obliged to leave the solitude he loved, and seek medical help somewhere. His final decision fitted the tenor of his life. He chose to go to Ubeda rather than to Baeza because "in Ubeda nobody knows me". He was received there very coolly because his presence added to the community's expenses. He died on December 13, 1591.

John's life is a commentary on the truth that no external force or circumstance has the power to chain the inner Spirit we have been given. And that Spirit was made to soar high and free. His life of poverty and persecution could have produced a bitter cynic. Instead it formed a compassionate mystic who was able to write: "Where there is no love, put love, and you will find love."

THE SOARING BIRD

It makes little difference whether a bird is tied by a thin thread or by a cord. For even if tied by thread, the bird will be prevented from taking off just as surely as if it were tied by cord – that is, it will be impeded from flight as long as it does not break the thread. Admittedly the thread is easier to rend, but no matter how easily this may be done, the bird will not fly away without first doing so.

John of the Cross, The Ascent of Mount Carmel

"Cut the string, friend, cut the string!"

In February 1990, the Melbourne papers reported the suicide of a man about to be released from prison. The 37-year-old man had been jailed for the murder of his father. Under the headline "Tragic killer scared to death of freedom", the article reported that in the 16 years he had been in prison, this man had never ever had a visitor, a letter or a phone call. He had become an institutionalised loner, who, when faced with freedom, had hung himself with an electric cord.

One cannot help contrasting the two men: John of the Cross who from his prison cell urges us to consider the image of a soaring bird, and the prisoner from Melbourne whose name also was John, who sees no way out in his life. One man ends his time of imprisonment with poems which sing of inner freedom and passionate love. The other ends his time of imprisonment by ending his life as well. It would be easy to see these two men as complete opposites. But it is not quite as simple as that. The difference between the two is not that one was scared of freedom and the other was not. John of the Cross also records that realising what real freedom meant was almost too much for him to bear. He wrote: "If his Majesty did not strengthen my weakness by a special help, it would be impossible to live."

Both men indeed experienced a fear of freedom. But one took the choice of certainty through death, while the other took the choice of risk through letting go into the unknown.

"Scared to death of freedom..." Yes, that's a good way of describing a human response. Many of us would have to admit that we are not too far from that response ourselves, even if we don't take the step that the tragic killer from Melbourne took. But there are ways of putting oneself to death without taking one's life. We can settle for a life that's safe, predictable, controlled and free of risk. That would be to settle for life on flat earth, when the invitation of Jesus is to fly free.

When you look at it, freedom is at the heart of Jesus' message. We are made to be free. This is what lies underneath all the words and actions of Jesus. He tells us that he has come so that we may have life and more life and more life. He likens his gift to springs of water which bubble up continuously, or to a breath of wind which blows where it wills, freely and often unpredictably. He says:

"If you make my word your home
you will indeed be my disciples.
You will learn the truth
and the truth will make you free."

And when you look closely you begin to realise that the problem Jesus had with the Scribes and Pharisees was not that they were evil, or full of malice, or even that they were deliberately closed to Jesus' invitation. It was just that they were, well, stuck. Stuck where they were, stuck with the need to be certain about everything, stuck even in their loyalty to their religion, stuck to the ground when they were really made for something different. "Look," they said to Jesus, "We've got Abraham, and we know who he was and where he came from. We've got Moses, and we know who he was and what he did for us. We've got the Law written down and we know what it means. We've got the Temple, and we have God in the Holy of Holies. We're quite happy about that because we're certain about these things. But you...? We don't know where you come from, or what your credentials are. We can't be certain that you, with your different slant, are right. What say we let go of the Law (which we are sure about) and follow you (whom we're not sure about), and then we discover that you are misguided? Where are we then? We'll have lost everything!"

And Jesus' response to all of this was not so much anger as sadness to the point of weeping. "If only you knew what was for your peace... but you wouldn't. If only... If only... But you wouldn't." Fortunately for us, some people did let Jesus free them, and so we can see what takes place when we experience that freedom. But then we notice two things immediately. First, we notice that all the characters whom Jesus set free were people who could afford to let go because they had nothing to lose: their reputation was gone, their standing with others was zero. It was Jesus or nothing. They were 'rock-bottom' people – the woman caught in the act of adultery; the man who had been born blind; the man who had been 38 years at the pool waiting for a cure. They had nothing to lose, and so they could afford to take the risk and let Jesus free them.

But the second thing we notice is what this freedom did to them. In an explosion of foolish energy, one man danced in the temple. Another ran through the crowd singing and calling out praises to the confusion of the bystanders. A woman bursts in on a social occasion, completely unannounced, and washes Jesus' feet. These foolish gestures could be done only by those who had felt an extraordinary weight falling off their shoulders – or to go back to our image, by those who felt that the cord which tied them was cut, and they were set free.

"Unbind him," said Jesus over Lazarus, "and let him go free." These are the words Jesus wants us to hear as we try to stare down the things that bind us. But when the chips are down, most of us are probably afraid of freedom. However much we struggle against losing our freedom, in the end we are probably even more afraid of the consequences of being really free.

When the walls of the communist dictatorship were crumbling in the Eastern-bloc countries, a journalist, commenting on the situation, said: "The people cannot live without freedom, but they don't realise how difficult it is to live with freedom."

The well-known parable in Dostoevsky's novel *The Brothers Karamazov* dramatically describes this struggle with true freedom. According to the story, Christ arrives in a town in Spain in the sixteenth century, and continues the work he did in Palestine. He heals the sick and sets people free from the things that burden them. The people recognise him and adore him, but he is arrested by the authorities of the Inquisition and sentenced to be burnt to death the next day. The Grand Inquisitor visits him in his cell to tell him that the Church no longer needs him. He accuses him of imposing on people the impossible burden of freedom. He says that Jesus should have given people no choice; then at least they would have had security. The Inquisitor tells Jesus that he, the Inquisitor, will be thanked for taking the responsibility for telling people what to do in conscience. The Inquisitor ends his speech: "I repeat, tomorrow You shall see that obedient flock who at a sign from me will hasten to heap up the hot cinders about the pile on which I shall burn You for coming to hinder us. For if anyone has ever deserved our fires, it is you. Tomorrow I shall burn you. I have spoken." Christ, who has been silent throughout the speech, walks to the Inquisitor and kisses him. No argument can overcome the kiss. The Inquisitor releases Christ but tells him to leave the city and never return. Christ, still silent, goes out into "the dark alleys of the city". As for the Inquisitor: "The kiss glows in his heart, but the old man adheres to his idea."

Living with freedom is a risky business, and perhaps only children can do that properly. When Jesus counselled Nicodemus to become like a child, Nicodemus rather scornfully reminded Jesus how difficult it would be to return to the mother's womb. Regressing physically wasn't what Jesus meant, but it's even harder to go back and recapture the inner spirit of a child.

There's a wonderful passage in the novel *Zorba the Greek* which sums it all up, really. The narrator is talking to Zorba:

"Perhaps I'll come along with you," I said, "I'm free."

Zorba shook his head.

"No, you're not free. The string you're tied to is perhaps longer than other people's. That's all. You're on a long piece of string, boss; you come and you go, and think you're free, but you never cut the string in two. And when people don't cut that string..."

"I'll cut it some day!" I said defiantly, because Zorba's words had touched an open wound in me and hurt.

"It's difficult, boss, very difficult. You need a touch of folly to do that: folly, don't you see? You have to risk everything! But you've got such a strong head; it'll always get the better of you. A man's head is like a grocer; it keeps accounts; I've paid so much and earned so much, and that means a profit of this much or a loss of that much! The head's a careful little shopkeeper; it never risks all it has, always keeps something in reserve. It never breaks the string."

He was silent, helped himself to some
more wine, but started to speak again.

"You must forgive me, boss," he said,
"I'm just a clodhopper. Words stick
between my teeth like mud to my boots.
I just can't turn out beautiful sentences and compliments. I just can't.
But you understand, I know."

He emptied his glass and looked at me.

"You understand!" he cried, as if suddenly filled with anger. "You
understand and that's why you'll never have any peace. If you didn't

understand, you'd be happy! What d'you lack? You're young, you
have money, health, you lack nothing. Nothing, by thunder! Except
just one thing – folly! And when that's missing, boss, well...."
He shook his head and was silent again.

I nearly wept. All that Zorba said was true. As a child I had been
full of mad impulses, superhuman desires. I was not content with
the world. Gradually, as time went by, I grew calmer. I set limits,
separated the possible from the impossible, the human from the
divine. I held my kite tightly so that it should not escape..." [81]

What God wants for us is to be free, and to live our lives with music in our soul. This is no far-away ideal, beyond human reach. The friends of God whose lives and experiences we've considered in this book, and so many thousands of others over the centuries, offer us proof that it is possible to let oneself fall into the arms of a loving God. And when that happens, what freedom of spirit there is!

Somewhere in my collection of favourite thoughts, I have kept this poem. I have no record of who wrote it, but I know it is based on John of the Cross' work, *The Ascent of Mount Carmel*.[82] The poem has encouraged and challenged me for a long time.

"From now on I'm always at his door
I gave away my heart and my fortune
I have no flock to shepherd any more
And there's no other work in my future.
My only occupation is love
Nothing else.

If friends ask for me
Tell them I'm off on an adventure
I'm lost on purpose
To be found by love."

As I read the poem I think I see John of the Cross looking at us across the centuries, and saying gently, but with his eyes piercing through our defences, "Cut the string, friend, cut the string!" He himself had done it, and he had found the foolish freedom of the friends of God.

The Author — Craig Larkin

A PERSONAL REFLECTION

BY SOPHIE JANSSENS

Craig Larkin was a special man, gifted with many talents and a combination of characteristics that one could easily consider as contrasting. He was intelligent and simple, profound, reflective and light, cheerful and disciplined, dynamic and stable, spiritual and concrete. I would add to this that he was strong but at the same time very conscious of his weakness, and he combined all these elements in a marvellous balance, and this and much more made him the special and lovely person he was. Sometimes he reminded me of a clown. He was a real Christian.

I had the privilege to know Craig from 2006, a few months after I started working for the General Administration of the Society of Mary based in Rome. Craig was the Vicar General, and when I started working he had just left Rome to receive medical care in New Zealand for problems with his back. I remember people talked often about him, and I was impressed by the fact that many people missed his presence. It was a first taste of what I would understand better later. If Craig was home, everybody just knew; and when he wasn't you missed his cheerful and energising presence.

"Woe to me if I do not proclaim the gospel" (1 Cor 9:16)

Craig never passed unobserved. He left traces everywhere he went. He loved life. He was interested in everything and he enjoyed detecting what was going on in somebody's mind. He searched for the good which is present in every person, and he loved to emphasise it. He loved drama! He enjoyed drama! He created drama! Nothing was boring with Craig, and even the most mundane meeting with him could become an exciting story. He talked with people he met on the street, in his gentle and cheerful style, and he usually left them with a smile on their face. He was very conscious of the creative power that every person possesses, and he sought not to be a pale or useless presence.

"Store up for yourselves treasures in heaven" (*Matthew 6:20*)

Craig didn't allow his life to be confined by conformism, and that made him free. But this kind of life demanded discernment and choices, and discipline as well. Craig was very well organised, business-like. He liked to "do things well". He was freely creative yet at the same time avoided leaving things to improvisation. When he finished his term as Vicar General in 2009, he was happy to have the time he needed to "accomplish" some important matters. Even if at that time there was no sign of his illness, he lived with the consciousness that time is not endless. Things had to be fulfilled, with a certain sense of haste, like the disciples of Emmaus who have to make haste to return to Jerusalem.

Being aware that he needed to nourish his mind with good food, he read a lot. He studied. But he knew that true wisdom is not only built by study, it's also made of human encounters, dialogue, relationships. So he travelled, to Greece, to Syria, to Turkey. He was intrigued by the experience and the traces of the Ancient Church, the Desert Fathers. He was particularly enamoured of the Orthodox world; he was attracted by their prayer and how they accepted mystery as part of reality.

The more time passed by, the more he felt the need for clear priorities, and the need to filter the things which were essential for him. Piece by piece, with patience, he gathered together a huge treasure of personal experiences which became wisdom to share. Amongst them were the spiritual inheritance of the Marist founder Jean-Claude Colin, the work on the Desert Fathers, prayer and, the letters from the Marist missionaries of Oceania.

He spent a significant part of his days in studying, elaborating, carefully selecting what was most essential. He saw all this in the light of a broader mission: making this inheritance available to many, and to facilitate for others the search for inner life. In this context one should see his dedication and his love for the work in the field of formation, and more particularly the formation of formators.

"Rejoice in hope, be patient in suffering, persevere in prayer" (**Rom 12:12**)

Craig loved to pray. He loved prayer in its mysterious beauty, and it became more important with the passing of the years. When life returned to its essentials, prayer became more important. Prayer and beauty were closely linked for him. He had a great sense to take care in the prayer and to make sure that it took place in the best way possible. The place had to be nice, carefully prepared, inviting for prayer, as a perfect choreography, because if everything was well prepared, there was space freed for the mystery to take place. No distractions from unexpected things going wrong. Time for silence too, and for symbols.

Symbols, and more generally images, were an important part of Craig's way of life. Even if he read a lot, he knew that symbols were stronger than words. "While we do forget words, we don't forget symbols", he said. So if a message is important, it's more fruitful to link it to a symbol (or an image). I remember Craig celebrating Mass, in a church in Ostia, as he often did, in the poor periphery of Rome. The church was packed with a variety of people: elderly women marked by time and fatigue, adults hardened by a life full of difficulties, young girls and boys growing up in the complexity of a life in a forgotten suburb of Rome, disabled persons. All of them assembled in the little church of Ostia, to receive the love and mercy of God, listening to Craig's words. It was Trinity Sunday, and Craig gave a very short and simple homily. Yes, I forgot his words, but I can still see him, teaching the whole congregation to make the symbol of Trinity with their fingers. "Come on," he said, "show me your hands, also the boys at the back." Some hesitated, but after a while every single person present in the church was showing proudly how they could make the symbol. I am convinced that most of them still remember.

"Rejoice that your names are written in heaven." (Luke 10:20)

In December 2013 – at that time he was leading a formation course for Marist confreres in Rome – Craig received the news that he was seriously ill. He decided to go back to New Zealand. He allowed himself one week to say goodbye. He had to say goodbye to the 'eternal city' which he had loved so much, goodbye to his many friends and contacts. He knew he would not come back. He decided to 'travel light', with only very important things. His sober lifestyle and his sense for the essential proved their value.

Despite the increasing discomfort of his illness, he continued working with his usual accurate, precise and disciplined rhythm, in the hope of accomplishing as much as possible. The doctors had talked about months, but Craig would live for more than one year and a half. In all this time his faith and his inner strength were as a beacon in the darkness. Craig had a great desire to live. He had loved and enjoyed life so much. Despite the suffering, he found peace, the peace of a man who had spent most of his life shaking off the superfluous to free energy to live always more in the light of the Lord.

> *Rejoice in the Lord always; again I will say, Rejoice. Let your gentleness be known to everyone. The Lord is near. Do not worry about anything, but in everything by prayer and supplication with thanksgiving let your requests be made known to God. And the peace of God, which surpasses all understanding, will guard your hearts and your minds in Christ Jesus.*

> *Finally, beloved, whatever is true, whatever is honourable, whatever is just, whatever is pure, whatever is pleasing, whatever is commendable, if there is any excellence and if there is anything worthy of praise, think about these things. Keep on doing the things that you have learned and received and heard and seen in me, and the God of peace will be with you.*

(Philippians 4: 4–9)

LOCATING THE MYSTICS

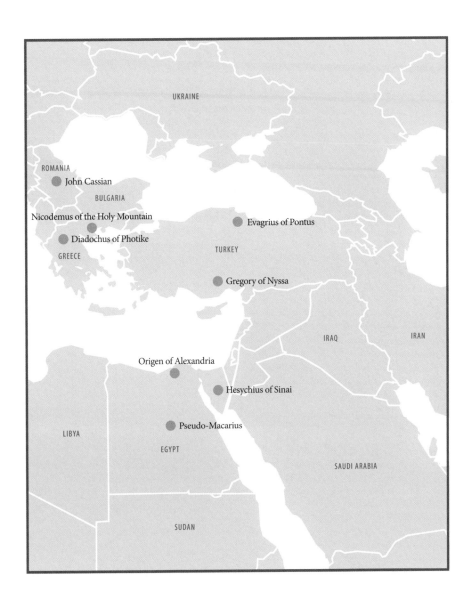

UKRAINE

ROMANIA

John Cassian

BULGARIA

Nicodemus of the Holy Mountain

Evagrius of Pontus

Diadochus of Photike

TURKEY

GREECE

Gregory of Nyssa

IRAQ

IRAN

Origen of Alexandria

Hesychius of Sinai

LIBYA

Pseudo-Macarius

EGYPT

SAUDI ARABIA

SUDAN

END NOTES

1   Psalm 41:10

2   Psalm 62:2

3   Sheila Upjohn, *In Search of Julian of Norwich* (London:Darton, Longman and Todd, 1987) p.12ff

4   This quote and story found in Maria L. Santa Maria *Growth through Meditation and Journal Writing* (Paulist Press, 1984) p.33

5   Sheila Upjohn, *In Search of Julian of Norwich* (London: Darton, Longman and Todd, 1985)

6   Nikos Kazantzakis, *Zorba the Greek* (United Kingdom: John Lehman, 1946) p.70

7   St Jerome, "Sermon on Psalm 41 addressed to the newly-baptised." (CCL 78,542-544) cf *Liturgy of the Hours: Office of Readings*, Thursday, thirteenth week in Ordinary Time

8   Guigo the Carthusian, *The Ladder of Monks*, Text 2

9   John Bunyan, *Pilgrim's Progress*, Part 1, "Author's Apology for his book." (London: Penguin Classics, 2008)

10   Anthony Coniaris, *Philokalia, the Bible of Orthodox Spirituality* (Minnesota: Light and Life Publishing, 1998) p.27

11   John Chrysostom, "Homily on the Second Letter to the Corinthians." Cf *Liturgy of the Hours* Vol 111, p. 346-7

12   John Climacus, *Ladder of Divine Ascent*, Step 30 (New York: Paulist Press, 1982)

13   Genesis 1:27

14   Athanasius, "Ad Adelphium 4" cf *De Incarnatione*, p. 54

15   William of Saint-Thierry, *Epistola ad Fratres de Monte Dei*, 258. English translation. *The Golden Epistle: A letter to the brethren at Mont Dieu.* (Cistercian Fathers Series 12, Spencer: 1971) p.94

16   Eulogy of Basil the Great, "Oration 43,48." pp. 26,560, Olivier Clement, *The Roots of Christian Mysticism*, p 56

17   Origen, *Commentary on St Matthew's Gospel*, 16, 23 (pp. 13, 1453) cf Clement, op cit p.76

18   Gregory of Nazianzen, *Oration 45, For Easter*, 7 (pp. 36,850)

19   Gregory of Nyssa, *Homilies on the Beatitudes*, 6 (pp. 44, 1270) cf Clement, op cit p.237

20   Gregory of Nyssa, *Second Homily on the Song of Songs* (pp. 44,765)

21   Leo the Great, *Homily 21 on the Nativity*

22   Romans 7:18

23   Romans 5:12

24   1 Cor 15:25-28

25 Benedicta Ward, *The Sayings of the Desert Fathers* Antony 2 (Cistercian Publications,1984) p.2

26 Psalm 19:15

27 Matt 22:37; Mk 12:30; Lk 10:27

28 Diadochus of Photike, "On Spiritual Discernment and Knowledge", in *Philokalia* Vol 1, p.287

29 Isaac of Nineveh, in *The Art of Prayer: An Orthodox Anthology*, Igumen Chariton ed, (London: Faber and Faber 1997) p.164

30 Mark the Ascetic, "Letter to Nicolas the Solitary", *Philokalia* Vol I p.159

31 Evagrius of Pontus, "On Prayer 149" in *Philokalia* Vol I, p.71

32 Palladius, "The Lausiac History" Trans. Robert T. Meyer in *Ancient Christian Writers No 34: The Works of the Fathers in Translation* (New York:Paulist Press, 1964), p.110

33 Benedicta Ward, *The Sayings of the Desert Fathers: The Alphabetical Collection* revised ed (Kalamazoo, Michigan: Cistercian Publications, 1984) p.64

34 St Augustine, Sermon 256

35 *Conferences* 1,2,1;1,4,1;2,11,7;2,26,4, cf Columba Stewart, *Cassian the Monk.* (Oxford University Press, 1998) p.207

36 Nehemiah 9:19-21

37 Evagrius of Pontus, *Praktikos*, 13 (Kalamazoo, Michigan:Cistercian Publications, 1981)

38 Hugh Trevor-Roper, *The Rise of Christian Europe* (New York: W.W. Norton and Company, 1966) p.165-66

39   Heb: 11:6

40 Alfred Lord Tennyson, The Higher Pantheism, 1, 11-12

41 Acts 17:28

42 Walter Hilton, *The Ladder of Perfection*, Chapter 24

43 Exodus 24:9,10

44 Exodus 19:18,20

45 Symeon the New Theologian, in *Writings from the Philokalia* p.131

46 Theophan the Recluse in *The Art of Prayer, an Orthodox Anthology*, compiled by Igumen Chariton on Valamo, (Faber and Faber, 1966) p.63

47 Preface: *A Handbook of Spiritual Counsel, Nicodemus of the Holy Mountain.* Trans. Fr Peter Chamberas, (New York: Paulist Press) p.10

48 Evagrius of Pontus, *Talking Back: A Monastic Handbook for Combating Demons.* Trans. David Brakke (Collegeville, Minnesota: Liturgical Press, 2009)

49 Mark 10:21

50 Ephesians 6:10

51 Romans 7:24

52 1 Peter 1:35

53 Philippians: 4:14

54 1 John 1:8, 2:2

55 Benedicta Ward, *The Sayings of the Desert Fathers, Antony* 27 (London: Mowbray Publishing, 1975)

56 "Barsanuphius the Elder, Questions and Answers" in Ware, *The Inner Kingdom* (New York:Vladimir's Press, 2000) p.120

57 Benedicta Ward, op cit *Antony 16*

58 Mark 10:46

59 Hesychius, "On Watchfulness and Holiness" in *Philokalia* Vol 1 (London:Faber and Faber 1979) p.193

60 Ibid., p.193

61 Ibid., p.186

62 John 14: 14

63 Acts 3:7

64 John 2:1-12

65 Mark 1:24

66 Mark 1:21

67 John 4:29

68 Mark 2:8

69 John 11

70 Mark 5:18;Luke 5:8

71 John 10:10

72 Matthew 28:10

73 Hesychius op cit p.197

74 Surin, J.J. *Correspondence*, Michel de Certeau, ed (Paris,1966) Letter 52, May 3 1635, p.263

75 Surin, J.J. *Triumphe de l'amour divine sur les puissances de l'enfer et science experimentale des choses de l'autre vie*, Michael de Certeau, ed (Grenoble: J. Millon, 1990) p.119

76 A. Poulain, "Jean-Joseph Surin" in *Catholic Encyclopaedia* Vol 14 (New York:Robert Appleton Company, 1912)

77 Letter of Pere Jacques Nau, quoted in: Svitlana Kobets, *Fools in Christ: East vs West*. Canadian-American Slavic Studies. Vol 34, no 3. Fall 2000, pp337-363

78 Francis Xavier Nguyen van Thuan, *Testimony of Hope* (Paulist Press, 2001)

79 Maisie Ward, *Caryll Houselander* (London: Sheed and Ward, 1962)

80 From *Lift up your hearts* (London: Sheed and Ward, 1978)

81 Nikos Kazantkzakis, *Zorba the Greek* (United Kingdom: John Lehman, 1946) p.303-304

82 St John of the Cross, *The Ascent of Mount Carmel*, Book 1, Chapter 11, paragraph 4